Pocket Workshop

ESSAYS ON LIVING AS A WRITER

Edited by Tod McCoy
& M. Huw Evans

HYDRA HOUSE
CLARION WEST WRITERS WORKSHOP

978-0-9979510-7-3 (trade paperback)
978-0-9979510-8-0 (limited edition hardcover)

Hydra House
2850 SW Yancy St. #106
Seattle, WA 98126
http://www.hydrahousebooks.com/

All essays contained herein are original to the collection with the exception of the following:

"Thickening the Plot," by Samuel R. Delany, first appeared in *Those Who Can*, ed. Robin Scott Wilson (New York: Mentor Books; New American Library, 1973).

"Some Thoughts on Exposition," by Tobias S. Buckell, is adapted for *Pocket Workshop* from "Expository Narrative" in *It's All Just a Draft* (Xenowealth Books, 2019).

"The Narrative Gift as a Moral Conundrum," © 2004 Ursula K. Le Guin. First appeared on UrsulaKLeGuin.com in 2004, and then in *No Time to Spare*, published by Houghton Mifflin Harcourt in 2018. Reprinted by permission of Curtis Brown, Ltd.

"Writing in the Age of Distraction," by Cory Doctorow, first appeared in *Locus* magazine (January 2009): http://www.locusmag.com/Features/2009/01/cory-doctorow-writing-in-age-of.html

Pitfalls of Writing Science Fiction & Fantasy: General Useful Information & Other Opinionated Comments by Vonda N. McIntyre (Book View Café, 2012). Reprinted by permission of Clarion West Writers Workshop, acting as agent for the Estate.

"Positive Obsession" copyright 1989 © by Octavia E. Butler. First published as "Birth of a Writer" in *Essence* magazine. Reprinted by permission of Writers House LLC acting as agent for the Estate.

COVER ART by Cory Skerry
BOOK DESIGN by John D. Berry

Contents

Forewords

For those unfamiliar with it, Clarion West is a writing workshop which provides instruction and insight into the art and craft of speculative fiction writing. The workshop has been operating continuously since 1984—a full thirty-five years at the time of this printing, fifty years since its origin in 1971.

Each summer, the Clarion West Writers Workshop, the flagship program, offers six weeks of in-residence instruction for eighteen students from around the world, with each week led by a different writer or editor from the fields of science fiction, fantasy, or horror. To date, more than 600 writers have passed through the summer program, many of whom have become professional writers or editors and are still active in the field.

But there's more than just writing instruction in the workshop. Living and working alongside so many like-minded people creates a sense of community, builds bonds with other writers, allows for experimentation in a safe environment, builds confidence, opens an awareness of the diversity of people, and offers a journeymanship into the field unlike most other writing workshops in existence. It is not JUST a writing workshop.

This book is intended to be a reflection of the workshop itself, a way to give back—by delivering thoughts and insights about writing and process from writers who have taught at Clarion West over the past thirty-five years—to members of our community who may not be able to attend the workshop. And what was originally conceived to literally fit "in your pocket" grew into a much larger tome. We apologize that all of this wisdom may not fit anymore.

Maybe you've made a sale, maybe you've written a draft or two of a novel, maybe you've made the decision that THIS profession is your calling, and you need more information to keep going. Maybe you're simply trying to get out of the slush pile. Within these pages you'll find advice distilled from nearly four decades of writing acumen. We hope they will nudge you forward and help you move on to the next level of your writing career.

We wish you the best of luck, and keep writing! Onward!

Tod McCoy, Editor
Clarion West Writers Workshop Chair
Publisher, Hydra House Books

Co-editing *Pocket Workshop* has been nearly as immersive and transformative as attending Clarion West, and I'm honored—and humbled—to have poured myself into the project.

Tod wrote about the book's *what*, *why*, and *for whom*, so I'll focus on *how*: specifically, how the essays are arranged (and how to spite our prescriptive sequencing and find your own best path).

We began with a nominally thematic scheme: pieces heavy on technique to the front (you're here to hone skills? cue the nuts and bolts); theoretical and philosophical essays following (what does it mean? how do you figure out what you *want* it to mean?); next, practical advice (research; get it right; use it well; keep on writing; keep on keeping on; don't get distracted; unblock yourself; pass it on); and finally, at the end, deep introspective musings on living as a writer (is your muse obsessed? are you lost? can writing save? what paves the road to *writers'* hell?).

It was a lovely idea, sorting the essays by type. Until it fell apart. Or, rather, together.

The more we read, the more each essay grew connected to every other. And they weren't just connected, but entangled, symbiotic. (Cory Skerry's mushrooms on the cover are the product of his own inspiration, but they complement my conceit: these essays are fruiting bodies of a great writerly mycelium.) I sometimes suspected the authors of conspiring. They'd all, independently, written pieces whose common threads (hyphae?) wove themselves into a single fabric, and we could no longer label any one essay as *only* "practical" or "theoretical" or "introspective."

So, we pondered, and shuffled, and unshuffled, and finally quit worrying and trusted our editorial guts. We settled on *a* right sequence—but it's not *the* right sequence. *The* right sequence is the one *you* follow. Ask yourself what you, as a writer, need. Consult the table of contents, select a toothsome title, take that first Alice-like nibble (yes, mushrooms again), and be affected.

OK, maybe I can help a little: Are you blocked? Read "Going Through an Impasse." Need a kickstart into your story? Tap "Tapping the Source," with a chaser of "We All Have to Start Somewhere." Doubting your story's logic or structure? Trust in "Coincidentally…" and "Setting the Scene." Obsessed with perfection? Indulge in "Thickening the Plot," "The Devil Is in the Details," and "Something to Cry About." Characters not cooperating? Get an assist from "Status" and "Neowise." Feeling generic? Look to "Channeling Voices." Pondering symbolism? Meditate on "The Old Marvellous." Or… perhaps *writing* has gone from your world; you're not alone. Run to the embrace of "*Take As Needed," and bask a while in "Matters of Life and Death."

Of course, if you choose to read the book start-to-finish, you'll be fine—"Being and Becoming a Writer" is a perfect beginning, "Proverbs of Hell for Writers," a marvelous dénouement—but do read what you need when you need it. Some essays may not speak to you (at first), while others sing in your mind for days or years. If you read a favorite dozens of times before you've read them all even once, well done. But as you eventually unpack the rest of this book's pieces, may each prove as vital and nourishing to your story as their whole has to mine.

M. Huw Evans, Editor

Introduction

NEILE GRAHAM

We have expectations about what we'll get in a book for writers. Some of us might be looking for reminders of our best workshop moments. Others might be dreaming of a taste of our future. We hope, of course, that inside the book we'll find the key to making our writing soar: the tools we need to launch a writing career with a solely upward trajectory. We want the book to include the in-group handshake only successful writers know and the blueprints for the decoder ring that will unlock the secret to brilliant writing and to building our most perfect writerly selves. However, you probably have enough experience to know that what you're going to get is tough-love reality slaps and some shivers of inspiration. Those are in here, but what you might not realize, is that reality slaps *are* the handshake and inspiration *is* the decoder ring.

These essays come from writers who have experienced the Clarion West Writers Workshop, as instructors, special guests, and often also as students. Clarion West and the few workshops like it know the power of gathering groups of writers together. It's especially powerful to gather together those who know enough to be dangerously excited—and dangerously scared—to meet, to be set free to talk about what they love with others who also love it. For many of them, it's the first time they've done that. Add to this a mix of instructors who are either a few leaps farther along the honored writing career path or have already reached many of their dreams and are exploring what comes next, and you have an unmistakable magic. What is said within the workshop's walls ranges from mechanics and craft to the business (emotional and practical) of being a writer, and beyond, to sheer glorious writerly revelation.

A taste of that power is in these pages. A strong, smoky peaty whisky taste of it. Some of it will be the calm flavor of knowledge you recognize, reinforcing things you already know. Some of it will warm your belly with ambition. Some of the rough edges will make your lips numb. And some of it will burn and tingle all the way through your core.

I have been at Clarion West with all of these writers. I've seen their intense hour-long sessions and one-day workshops, and for twenty summers—first as a student myself and then, for nineteen years, helping to lead the team running Clarion West's workshops—I experienced the six-week gathering of writers, the sweating out the words of stories, the terror and joy of being taken seriously in a critique, the struggle of giving honest critiques, and the wonder of hearing what other writers have to share.

These essays all have important things to say to you. People say writing cannot be taught. That looks true from certain angles and from others it sounds like the sheerest bullshit. What is undeniably true is that writers and writing can always get stronger. Writers and their stories can always be more, get better, dig deeper, wax wiser. Sometimes it's by building up to a greater richness and sometimes it's by paring down to simplicity. That's probably the greatest truth I learned from the writers in these pages.

Here's what you'll find in this book: how tough writing is—and how worthwhile. Writing is all sorcery and inference, bespelling the reader, bespelling *you*, the author and creator. No, wait, it's tearing *off* the glamour to reach the bones of the tale you're telling. Here you'll find nuts and bolts, different ways of getting into looking at story. You'll find flow and conversation between the essays, no matter which order you read them. (This is something I learned watching the six-week workshop for so many years—there is always a flow, a shape that the whole collection of weeks takes, and somehow there still would be, no matter what order they land in.) You'll find some ideas that reinforce your own, some that show yours from differing angles, some that contradict both yours and the ideas presented by others within this book. Some of the ideas here sidle up sideways to sneak up on truths. Sometimes we have to re-imagine what we know to see it clearly. A couple of these essays may help you with that.

After reading this collection and confronting such ideas myself, I trust that what happened for me will happen for you—that inside these pages you'll both recognize some ideas you've wanted and discover (and understand) less familiar ones you never knew you needed. Some will resonate with you. Some will help you as you travel farther along in your career. I hope you'll find some challenges and find ideas that make you think and imagine new things, that you might look back on as something that helped make the path ahead a little clearer, or a little messier—and more true.

Take a sip. Stretch your wings. Get ready to launch, whether it's for the first or the hundredth time. It's a hell of a lot of work to keep flying, but these words will help you see how it can be done.

NEILE GRAHAM is Canadian by birth and inclination, but currently lives in Seattle, USA, where she attended Clarion West then helped run the program from 2001 through 2019. In 2017 she won a World Fantasy Award for that work. Neile's poetry and fiction have been published in the US, the UK, Canada, and now all over the internet. She has four full-length poetry collections, most recently *The Walk She Takes*, and a spoken word CD, *She Says: Poems Selected and New*. For more information, see neilegraham.com.

Being and Becoming a Writer

KAREN LORD

Writing advice ranges from broadly universal to deeply individual. Tools that work wonders for one book, or story, or writer may fail utterly for another. Some writers need company in the form of workshops or critique groups; others can only create solo, at least until that first, mad, messy draft is entirely done. You learn to choose what works when it works and find your own path to your destination. There's plenty of material on craft to sift through.

Less common, but perhaps more necessary, are the tips and techniques that have nothing to do with writing and everything to do with creating an environment in which writing can happen. Again, these range from the general to the specific. A professional writer in the Caribbean is not going to have the same experiences and resources as a professional writer in the USA. But we do have similar challenges in this global publishing industry, and if you don't pay attention to what writers say at different stages of their careers—those ten-, twenty-, and thirty-year veterans—you will miss out on a lot of marvelous insights that will help you stay the course for the long haul.

Here are the things I knew early, and the things I wish I had known earlier. This is what came naturally, and what I'm still working through. As with the craft, choose what works when it works, and leave the rest alone.

Talent will take you only so far. The gap between being an amateur and being a professional is very wide. Talent helps, beyond a doubt, but there are plenty of obstacles on the way from talent to profit. Fortunately, transferable skills from any professional field will help: the ability to schedule work, meet deadlines, and communicate clearly; a basic knowledge of accounting and taxes; maintaining work/life balance (or dual-job balance); negotiating skills; and teamwork. Learning the quirks of the publishing industry of your region will take time and effort, but also *saves* time and effort in the long run, when it comes to selecting an agent, attending literary festivals, and committing to projects.

"Don't quit your day job" isn't an insult. It's a valuable piece of advice. You don't have to make all your money from writing to call yourself a professional. There are many award-winning writers of the highest caliber who are not pulling in six-figure salaries from their work. Perhaps they work slowly, perhaps they work in a genre or form that isn't lucrative, or perhaps they genuinely like their day jobs and find their muse there as well.

The 'starving/suffering artist' myth is dangerous. Do not believe it. Although trauma can be converted into unforgettable literature, that is usually after the fact. Writing in the midst of crisis is a miserable and difficult task. Try to organize your life so you can focus on your work without worrying about your body, your mind, or your life falling to pieces while you're distracted.

The way you read, and the way you feel about reading, may change. Instead of becoming immersed in the story, you may find your suspension of disbelief getting tangled up in the workings of your critical brain. This is normal, although it may feel distressing at first. Now you're primed to look at the story as a piece of workmanship rather than simply content to consume. Don't fight it, embrace it. Figure out what your favorite and not-so-favorite authors can teach you.

Carve out time to keep learning. Whether it's about a city, a historical era, or a branch of science, any input of new knowledge keeps your creative well fresh. Stories need research, and they also need a lived life to interpret them. Travel, train, expand your experiences, and stretch your mind.

Read everything around you. But remember that stories are not found only in words. They can be found in a garden, or a work of abstract art. Learn to identify story structures in various media, and see what riffing off those structures can bring to your writing.

Take a break and put the manuscript (or book) down. Do writers even have holidays? What is recreation but a shift from the norm and the everyday? And what can you do when books were once your recreation but are now your job? Fortunately for you, you have already taken the advice in the previous paragraph and learned to find stories elsewhere!

Pick a new hobby. Don't even try to be good at it. Everyone needs a no-pressure activity they can feel free to fail at. Join a hike club, play a team sport, form a band. Do anything that gets you away from writing and into using your mind and body in other ways.

Find workmates. Writing can be solitary work. Collaborations, team projects and shared marketing/networking make it less solitary. You will be exposed to unanticipated challenges, fresh thoughts, and new skills. Recreation isn't always doing something different; sometimes it can be doing the same thing in different ways.

Don't be afraid to write more slowly, or stop writing entirely. (See above: *don't quit your day job.*) A hiatus isn't a tragedy. It might be another way to refill the creative well. It might also be the end of your writing career—and that's not always a bad thing. Writers have been known to happily shift their career path to teaching, editing, or directing—all still within creative fields.

Writers have also left the arts entirely when they feel they have nothing left to say and they are satisfied with what they have already produced. The work still stands, and if the writer is fortunate and the work has merit, it will stand the test of time. Which would you rather write: one book that takes two decades to write, but is loved and remembered for half a millennium; or twenty novels over twenty years that never make a splash, but steadily pay your bills? (It is not a trick question. Both are valid goals. Prolific writers can produce excellent books, mediocre writers can write slowly, and anyone's work can go out of print regardless of quality.)

The publishing industry is a capricious beast. Money, awards, and fame do not come to many, and are not the reward of only the deserving. Accept that, and write for the sake of writing, because, like goodness, the well-crafted story is its own reward. Write like it's your calling, and write like it's your job. But above all, live as if you plan to write for years and years to come.

KAREN LORD is a Barbadian author, editor, and research consultant. Her debut novel, *Redemption in Indigo*, won several awards and was nominated for the 2011 World Fantasy Award for Best Novel. Her other works include the science fiction novels *The Best of All Possible Worlds* and *The Galaxy Game* and the crime-fantasy novel *Unraveling*. She edited the anthology *New Worlds, Old Ways: Speculative Tales from the Caribbean*. She was a judge for the 2019 Commonwealth Short Story Prize and the 2018 CODE Burt Award for Caribbean YA Literature. She has taught at the 2018 Clarion West Writers Workshop and the 2019 Clarion Workshop, and she co-facilitated the 2018 Commonwealth Short Story Prize Workshop in Barbados. She has been a featured author at literary festivals from Adelaide to Edinburgh to Berlin, and often appears at the Bocas Lit Fest in Trinidad & Tobago.

We All Have to Start Somewhere: Finding Your Process and Making it Work for You

TINA CONNOLLY AND CAROLINE M. YOACHIM

Introduction. When we were planning our first class together (a one-day workshop about writing a complete story from start to finish), we quickly discovered that we approach story creation very differently. Caroline generally starts from a concept or abstract idea, and Tina tends to start from character or emotion. Although at first this led to confusion about how we should structure the class, it quickly became the focus of our co-teaching method, because we could provide a wide variety of methods for how to get into a story, how to finish a story, and what to do when you get stuck.

Some people might know early on what kind of writer they are, but others (Tina!) really have no idea for honestly quite the longest time. Spending some time thinking about your writing process can help identify the parts that are easier or more challenging as you work your way to a completed story.

One of the interesting ideas that emerged from this first class was the realization that we wanted to use the terms "character-driven" and "plot-driven" in a whole new way. It can be misleading to think of a finished story in these terms, since stories (in general) should have both characters and plot. *But!* These categories can be an invaluable tool in thinking about how *you personally* dive into constructing your story. By the end of the project, you want to have interesting characters that appear to drive a plot forward. How you get to that point—which things come first (or naturally) and which things you have to work to layer in second—that's totally up to you as a writer.

Tina: Starting from character. My stories tend to start more from loose noodling around on a character, bit of dialogue, or emotion. (I am also largely a pantser, though I try to think a lot more about outlines these days than I used to.) At any rate, this means that if someone gives me an idea-based prompt like "write a story about a new waste-management technology,"

I say, huh? But if someone says, "write about a sentient garbage truck," I say, oh yeah, I can totally start imagining that character.

Many people told me I was a character writer, and as a person with an acting background that felt viscerally true. But I still didn't understand why an idea-based prompt did absolutely nothing for me and, in fact, made me feel like a broken writer. It simply wasn't giving my character-obsessed brain anything to latch onto. And when I read plot-focused suggestions I felt equally confused. Someone tried to explain the idea of a "plot coupon" story to me—i.e., a straightforward story where the character collected, say, their sword and their shield and their potion, and then they fought the enemy and won. And that made zero intuitive sense to me, because *why* did they do all of those things? Knowing a *list* of plot steps did not help me write them. I had to know *why* my character cared before I could do anything at all.

So once I figured out what being a character-driven writer meant, it allowed me to understand what I needed, at every stage, to move through my story.

How do you know if you're a character-driven writer? This might be your process if:

- The thing that interests you the most about a story is the characters—digging into the study of what makes all these people tick, and watching them bounce off of each other.
- Characters frequently just start "talking in your head." They come out of nowhere, flounce onto the page, and declare that the rest of the story is about them. (Entertaining! Maddening!)
- You make progress through the draft by focusing on the protagonist's journey. It makes intuitive sense to think about the overall story as a series of choices that the protagonist is making. Your ending is likely intrinsically related to the moment where the character has made that big choice, that big change.
- You get stuck on the idea of plot, since the stuff that actually *happens* is secondary to the emotional journey the

> character's on. I often have brackets that are like [plot thing goes here]. If I'm not paying attention, my characters might sit around and have witty banter in lieu of actually *doing* something.

When I get stuck/blocked, it usually means I have lost sight of what the character wants. Knowing the character's overarching "I want" is what pulls me through the story. If I don't know what they want, then they stop moving. It took me a long time to figure this out, but now it's an invaluable tool for me to figure out how to get unblocked again. Once I know what they want, they will start naturally wanting to do things, and that will pull me forward again.

Another trick I use sometimes is to come up with a basic structure that I can then map the character's journey onto — a task list, perhaps, or a ticking clock. Ironically, once I figured this out, it meant I suddenly understood how to use "plot coupons." That is, if I know the character has to complete five tasks on a list, then I have a basic structure to follow while they have their character journey. The trick, for me, is that I need to understand *why* they want to complete that list. If they've got the drive, then I can follow them along that path.

Caroline: Starting from idea. When I first started out, there was a lot of writing advice that simply did not click for me. Think about what your character wants, and the story will unfold as they actively pursue their goal. Introduce obstacles that prevent them from attaining that goal. These are excellent pieces of advice and I can completely see the logic behind them — except that when I am writing I don't start with a character.

I start with an idea.

Oftentimes that idea is the core concept of the story. For instance, in "The Archronology of Love," I started from the question: what if we had the ability to dig through layers of time the way archaeologists dig through dirt? A large part of my process is figuring out how to populate that idea with characters. Basically, I need to bring the idea from an abstract level to a personal level. But how?

The trick, for me, is to stay focused on the idea. What aspects of the idea do I want to highlight in the story? For "The Archronology of Love," I wanted to show that sometimes the process of manipulating data destroys it. I also wanted to look at the relationship between perception, memory, and reality. Furthermore, I was interested in the ways that we construct narratives—how does the storyteller influence the story?

How do you know if you're an idea-driven writer? This might be your process if:

- The thing that interests you most about a story is abstract ideas: scientific concepts, philosophical debates, the underpinnings of magic systems, etc.
- You make progress through the draft by thinking about a sequence of interesting events rather than focusing on characters.
- You sometimes get stuck figuring out how to populate your cool alien or fantasy world with specific individual characters.
- Characters rarely (or never) start talking to you in your head, and they also rarely (or never) wander off and do things you don't want them to.

When I sit down to start drafting a story, I generally have several pages of rambling notes about very abstract ideas, often in the form of questions I think are interesting. Only then do I start thinking about how individual people might fit into the story—and even then, it is not about what the characters want or do not want. It is about what I need the characters to *do* in order to showcase some aspect of the idea. Basically, I start with plot puppets.

BUT WAIT, AREN'T PLOT PUPPETS BAD? In a finished story, people will sometimes criticize a story for having characters that are plot puppets. What they mean by this criticism tends to center around two things: implausible character motivations and character actions that are too predictable based on the plot. Which are valid criticisms in a finished piece. Ultimately, a finished story should have well-developed characters, an interesting plot, cool world-building, fascinating ideas, powerful emotions, etc., etc. But you don't have to do everything in the first draft.

Character motivation is an issue I often deal with in revisions. I don't create a character and then think about what that specific individual might want; instead I reverse engineer the character at the end to make it seem realistic that they'd do what I need them to do to drive the plot and showcase the ideas.

Integrating all the parts. A lot of writing is about finding your own process. What is it that draws you to a certain story? Do you start with a distinctive voice, or an intriguing character? Do you find yourself more drawn to an interesting scientific or philosophical concept, or maybe you love to build fantasy worlds? The starting point that sparks our interest in a story varies from one writer to the next, and the process that gets us from that spark to a completed story also varies. The writing processes we've described here are just two of the many possible ways to go from that first spark of excitement to a finished story.

A finished project combines a number of elements—characters and ideas, world-building, voice, theme, plot—but the process of getting everything into the story can vary greatly from one writer to the next. Identifying your own process, thinking about what comes intuitively *to you*, can be helpful in knowing how to start, what to do when you get stuck, and trouble spots to look for in revisions. Tina's tips on character might be most useful for character-driven writers when they are working on a first draft ... but those tips can also help idea-driven writers trying to fix character arcs during revisions. Likewise for Caroline's tips on starting from an idea.

And one final tip: it can be super helpful to find a beta reader who approaches things from an angle opposite to your own, to spot what you might have overlooked. And vice versa! At the very least, it might spawn many late-night conversations that start with "Wait, how do you write a story again???"

TINA CONNOLLY's books include the Ironskin trilogy (Tor), the Seriously Wicked series (Tor Teen), and the collection *On the Eyeball Floor and Other Stories* (Fairwood Press). She has been a finalist for the Hugo, Nebula, Norton, Locus, and World Fantasy awards. She is one of the co-hosts of *Escape Pod*, and runs the flash fiction podcast *Toasted Cake*. Find her at tinaconnolly.com.

CAROLINE M. YOACHIM is a prolific author of short stories, appearing in *Lightspeed*, *Beneath Ceaseless Skies*, *Clarkesworld*, and *Uncanny*, among other places. She has been a finalist for the World Fantasy, Locus, Sturgeon, and multiple Hugo and Nebula Awards. Yoachim's collection *Seven Wonders of a Once and Future World & Other Stories* and her award-nominated novelette "The Archronology of Love" are available from Fairwood Press. Find her online at carolineyoachim.com.

Setting the Scene

NANCY KRESS

Imagine you are a director mounting a play. Unless you are going the Shakespearian, totally bare stage route, one of your first jobs is to decide how the stage will look: modern multi-platformed with perhaps a few chairs? A fully designed interior/exterior stage set? What furniture/trees/doorways do you need and where should they go?

This is the usual meaning of "setting the scene" and, of course, fiction writers do it, too, with description and sensory details. But the phrase has another meaning as well: Where do you place ("set") your scenes in relation to each other?

The scene is the basic building block of fiction, and how you position one scene relative to another greatly affects how the reader receives your story. In addition, each kind of scene—I'm somewhat arbitrarily deciding there are seven—has different requirements for both content and placement.

The opening scene. This goes—duh!—at the beginning. In most commercial fiction, it is fully dramatized, which means it has a beginning, middle, and end, and it features characters interacting with each other. There are exceptions to this: N. K. Jemisin's novel *The Fifth Season* begins with an expository stretch in which the author speaks directly to the reader ("Let's start with the end of the world, why don't we?"). A strong authorial voice can make this work. In general, however, an opening scene best captures the reader's attention when it does all of the following:

- Starts with an arresting first sentence ("The sky above the port was the color of television, tuned to a dead channel," from William Gibson's *Neuromancer*)
- Includes characters both performing actions and talking to each other

- Shows us (rather than tells us) through sensory details where and when we are: A medieval hut? The bridge of a spaceship? A ruined future New York? Mars?
- Includes some conflict, even if at this point it is minor, or else promises conflict to come
- Ends with something that makes us want to keep reading. This is usually some variation of the dramatic question "And what will the characters do about *that*?"

Other dramatized scenes. These make up the bulk of most commercial fiction. They include the same elements as the opening scene, plus the requirement that we need to know the scene's relationship to the previous one. How much time has elapsed? Is it in the same place, or have you switched locations? If this story is being told in multiple third person, whose point of view are we in now? Get this information into the first few paragraphs of the scene, so we can concentrate on what is happening instead of trying to figure out when, where, and to whom it is happening.

Dramatized scenes can be either quiet or action-filled. In quieter scenes, two or more people might be discussing plans, or the point-of-view character might be thinking over the situation, or someone might be traveling somewhere (although be wary of including much "locomotion writing" unless we really need to know that your protagonist took the Number 9 subway uptown and then walked four blocks east). Effective quiet scenes often end with something interesting, such as a decision, a new plan, or a new piece of information introduced into the plot.

Action scenes include, well, action: loud arguments, violence, chases, sex, presidential elections, Mars landings, tornadoes, births, deaths, weddings, etc.

It is important to not have too many of each kind in a row. Too many low-key scenes following each other, and the tension of your story dissipates. Too many high-stakes action scenes can work better, but can also feel too frenetic, as if the author is trying to substitute sheer movement for story development. Vary the energy levels of your scenes. This is where a beta reader is invaluable: they can tell you "Here it started to drag for me" or

"So much was happening that I lost track of what the characters are feeling."

The dreaded expository lump. The expository scene isn't really a scene at all: It's a section of information that the author has decided we need to know. It isn't dramatized because the characters already know it, or because having one character explain the stardrive, the political situation, or the history of dragons to another seems too contrived.

Exposition has a bad rap. It is considered to interrupt the story's flow (true) and to be boring (not necessarily). If you have only a paragraph or so of exposition, just drop it in there; the reader will hardly notice. Sometimes, however, you need or want to explain something important at length: why society periodically falls apart (*The Fifth Season*), what robots can and cannot do (Asimov's Three Laws), how resource distribution works in a complex society set on an inhospitable moon (*The Dispossessed*, Ursula K. Le Guin).

If so, just go ahead and create an expository lump. The reader will not object *if* you place the exposition correctly. Put it:

- After you've created a plot reason to tell us the information. In *The Fifth Season*, society *has* just fallen apart (along with the planet's crust) and so we're interested in why. Asimov's robots are doing something—how much can they get away with? Le Guin's society is in a drought, and when there is not enough to go around, resource distribution becomes critical.
- Second, follow the Kress Swimming Pool Theory of Fiction. If you cannot dive (and I cannot), then you push off from the side of the pool. If you are lazy (I am) and you push off hard, you will get to glide before you have to start pumping arms and legs. An exciting, action- or conflict-filled dramatic scene is a "push" to the narrative. You can then "glide" with a section of exposition without losing reader interest.

Place your expository lumps after exciting scenes.

The summary scene. A summary scene contains action that you don't want to dramatize, so you just summarize it. Perhaps this same situation has occurred before, when you did dramatize it, so you just want a brief (but interesting) note to the reader that, yes, Mary and John are fighting again about his mother's interfering, this time because she interfered with something different from last time. Or the travelers are crossing their third stretch of desert and are getting weaker. Or your starship captain is once again going through his morning routine to try to hide signs of his hangover before his officers realize he is too impaired to command.

Another use of the summary scene is to foreshadow something that will happen later. You want to get Chekhov's gun plausibly in place so it can fire later, but not spend too much time on it now. Summarize the scene where your character buys it and sticks it over that mantel (metaphorically or not).

The summary scene, like a chunk of exposition, works best when it's placed after a more fully developed scene in which something exciting happens. It also needs at least a few fresh, sharp details so we can visualize it. It *is* a scene, albeit a tiny one.

The flashback. A flashback scene is a dramatized scene of events that occurred before the main story began. Whatever happens in the scene is interesting and important enough that you want it dramatized, not just summarized or given in exposition. But because a flashback, like summary and expository scenes, occurs out of story time, it will interrupt the story's flow by yanking us back in time. Minimize the disruptive effect by following the same guidelines as for exposition: Create a need in the reader to know what happened before, and try to place the flashback after an exciting scene that accomplishes that.

Suppose, for example, that you have two people in a scene who clearly dislike—maybe even hate—each other, and they must work together to address some dire situation. After their dislike is clear, the reader will wonder why there is so much tension between them. That's when the ground has been prepared to show that ten years ago, she blew up a planet he was fond of.

Because the ground needs to be prepared, it's usually not a good idea to place a flashback too close to the opening. We need to be interested in your characters' present before we can care about their pasts.

The climax. This is where all the forces opposing each other come together, whether those forces are two armies, two people, or two warring values within an individual. (Or all three in the same work.)

Placement of the climax is important. After it occurs, the story is essentially resolved, so it should be placed near, or even right at, the end. If it comes too soon, the rest of the work will drain away the satisfying resolution of tension that a climax should bring (which is why too much verbiage after the big scene is labeled "anti-climactic").

Nor should a climax speed by too fast. Your story has built to this point; give it enough words to justify all that build-up. And, of course, it should not occur offstage. Whoever wins or loses in your story, and whatever price they must pay for either, we need to see it fully and in detail.

The denouement. Contrary to what I just said, this does come after the climax. It is what Mark Twain called "the marryin' and the buryin'"—where we find out what happened to everybody, assuming you haven't already accounted for them all. The classic denouement from childhood is "And they lived happily ever after." It's Luke Skywalker and Han Solo receiving their medals, King Arthur's body being taken to Avalon. A short story, and some novels, may not need a denouement at all. If your work does, keep it as brief as you can.

Disclaimer. You can find stellar works of science fiction and fantasy that flout these guidelines (so can I). Writing is an art, not a science, and art has infinite variations. So consider these descriptions of scene placement not as rules, but as the usual signposts on the road to a successful story. And if you prefer to take a different road: May the fictional wind be at your back, and the literary sun shine on you.

NANCY KRESS is the author of thirty-five books, including twenty-seven novels, four collections of short stories, and three books on writing. Her work has won six Nebulas, two Hugos, a Sturgeon, and the John W. Campbell Memorial Award. Her most recent works are a stand-alone novella, *Sea Change* (Tachyon, 2020), and an SF novel of power and money, *The Eleventh Gate* (Baen, 2020). Nancy's fiction has been translated into more than a dozen languages, including Klingon, none of which she can read. Kress lives in Seattle with her husband, writer Jack Skillingstead.

Thickening the Plot

SAMUEL R. DELANY

I distrust the term "plot" (not to mention "theme" and "setting") in discussions of *writing*: it (and they) refers to an effect a story produces in the *reading*. But writing is an internal process writers go through (or put themselves through) in front of a blank paper that leaves a detritus of words there. The truth is, practically nothing is known about it. Talking about plot, or theme, or setting to a beginning writer is like giving the last three years' movie reviews from the Sunday *New York Times* to a novice filmmaker. A camera manual, a few pamphlets on matched action, viable cutting points, and perhaps one on lighting (in the finished film, the viewer hardly ever sees the light sources, so the reviewer can hardly discuss them, but their placement is essential to everything from mood to plain visibility) would be more help. In short, a vocabulary that has grown from a discussion of effects is only of limited use in a discussion of causes.

A few general things, however, can be noted through introspection. Here is an admittedly simplified description of how writing strikes me. When I am writing I am trying to allow/construct an image of what I want to write about in my mind's sensory theater. Then I describe it as accurately as I can. The most interesting point I've noticed is that the *writing down* of words about my imagined vision (or at least the choosing/arranging of words to write down) causes the vision itself to change.

Here are two of the several ways it changes:

First—it becomes clearer. Sudden lights are thrown on areas of the mental diorama dark before. Other areas, seen dimly, are revised into much more specific and sharper versions. (What was vaguely imagined as a green dress, while I fix my description of the light bulb hanging from its worn cord, becomes a patterned, turquoise print with a frayed hem.) The notation causes the imagination to resolve focus.

Second—to the extent that the initial imagining contains an action, the notating process tends to propel that action forward (or sometimes backward) in time. (As I describe how Susan, both hands locked, side-punched Frank, I see Frank grab his belly in surprise and stagger back against the banister—which will be the next thing I look at closely to describe.) Notating accurately what happens *now* is a good way to prompt a vague vision of what happens *next*.

Let me try to indicate some of the details of this process:

I decide, with very little mental concretizing, that I want to write about a vague George who comes into a vague room and finds a vague Janice ...

Picture George outside the door. Look at his face; no, look closer. He seems worried ...? Concerned ...? No. Look even closer and write down just what you see: *The lines across his forehead deepened.* Which immediately starts him moving. What does he do? ... *He reached for the* ... doorknob? No. Be more specific ... *brass doorknob. It turned* ... easily? No, the word "brass" has cleared the whole knob-and-lock mechanism. Look harder and describe how it's actually turning ... *loosely in its collar.* While he was turning the knob, something more happened in his face. Look at it; describe it: *He pressed his lips together*—No, cross that line out: not accurate enough. Describe it more specifically: *The corners of his mouth tightened.* Closer. And the movement of the mouth evoked another movement: he's pressing his other hand against the door to open it. (Does "press" possibly come from the discarded version of the previous sentence? Or did wrong use of it there anticipate proper use here? No matter; what does matter is that you look again to make sure it's the accurate word for what he's doing.) *He pressed his palm against the door* ... And look again; that balk in his next movement ... *twice, to open it.* As the door opens, I hear the wood give: *You could hear the jamb split*—No, cross out "split," that isn't right ... *crack*—No, cross that out too; it's even less accurate. Go back to "split" and see what you can do; listen harder ... *split a little more.* Yes, that's closer. He's got the door open, now. What do you see? *The paint*—No, that's not paint on the wall. Look harder: *The wallpaper was some color between green and gray.* Why can't you see it more clearly? Look around the rest of the room. Oh, yes: *The tan shade was drawn.* What about Janice? She was one of the first things you saw when the door opened. Describe her as you saw her: *Janice sat on the bed* ... no, more accurately ... *the unmade bed.* No, you haven't got it yet ... *Janice sat at the edge of the bed on a spot of bare mattress ticking.* No, no, let's back up a little and go through that again for a precise description of the picture you see: *Janice sat on the bare mattress ticking, the bedding piled loosely around her.* Pretty good, but the bedding is not really in "piles" ... *the bedding loose around her.* Closer. Now say what you have been aware of all the time you were wrestling to get that description right: *Light from the shade-edge went up her shoulder and cheek like tape.* Listen: George is about to speak: "*What are you doing here ...?*" No, come on! That's not it. Banal as they are, they may be the words he says, but watch him more closely while he says them. "*What—*" *he paused, as though to shake his head; but the only movement in his face was a shifting*—Try again: ... *a tightening* ... Almost; but once more ... *a deepening of the lines, a loosening of the lip*—"*are you doing here?*" Having gotten his expression more accurately, now you can hear a vocal inflection you missed before: "*are you* doing *here?*" There, that's much closer to what you really saw and heard. What has Janice just done? *She uncrossed her legs but did not look at him.* Ordinary grammar rules say that because the sentence's two verbs have one subject, you don't need any comma. But her uncrossing her leg and not looking up go at a much slower pace than proper grammar indicates. Let's make it: *She uncrossed her legs, but did not look at him ...*

Now let's review the residue of all that, the admittedly undistinguished, if vaguely noirish bit of prose the reader will have:

> The lines across his forehead deepened. He reached for the brass doorknob. It turned loosely in its collar. The corners of his mouth tightened. He pressed his palm against the door, twice, to open it. You could hear the jamb split a little more.
>
> The wallpaper was some color between green and gray. The tan shade was drawn. Janice sat on the bare mattress

ticking, the bedding loose around her. Light from the shade-edge went up her shoulder and cheek like tape.

"What—" he paused, as though to shake his head; but the only movement in his face was a deepening of the lines, a loosening of the lips—"are you *doing* here?"

She uncrossed her legs, but did not look at him.

And if you, the writer, want to know what happens next, you must take your seat again in the theater of imagination and observe closely till you see George's next motion, hear Janice's first response, George's next words, and Janice's eventual reply.

A reader, asked to tell the "plot" of even this much of the story, might say, "Well, this man comes looking for this woman named Janice in her room; he finds the door open and goes in, only she doesn't talk at first."

That's a fair description of the reading experience. But what *we* started with, to *write*, was simply: George goes into a room and finds Janice. (George, notice, at this point in the story hasn't even been named.) The rest came through the actual envisioning/notating process, from the interaction of the words and the vision. Most of the implied judgments that the reader picks up—the man is looking *for* Janice; it is *Janice's room*—are simply overheard (or, more accurately, overseen) suppositions yielded by the process itself. Let's call this continuous, developing interchange between imagination and notation, the *story process*; and let us make that our topic, rather than "plot."

A last point about our example before we go on to story process itself: by the time we have gone as far as we have with our "story," all this close observation has given us a good deal more information than we've actually used. Though I didn't when I began (to momentarily drop my editorial stance), I now have a very clear picture of George's and Janice's clothing. I've also picked up a good deal about the building they are in. As well, I've formed some ideas about the relationship between them. And all of this would be rescrutinized as I came to it, via the story process, were I writing an actual story.

The general point: the story process keeps the vision clear and the action moving. But if we do not notate the vision accurately, if we accept some phrase we should have discarded, if we allow to stand some sentence that is not as sharp as we can make it, then the vision is not changed in the same way it would have been otherwise: the new sections of the vision will not light up quite so clearly, perhaps not at all. As well, the movement of the vision — its action — will not develop in the same way if we put down a different phrase. And though the inaccurate employment of the story process may still get you to the end of the tale, the progress of the story process, which eventually registers in the reader's mind as "the plot," is going to be off: an inaccuracy in either of the two story process elements, the envisioning or the notation, automatically detracts from the other. When they go off enough, the progress of the story process will appear unclear, or clumsy, or just illogical.

It has been said enough times so that most readers have it by rote: a synopsis cannot replace a story. Nor can any analysis of the symbolic structure replace the reading experience that exposes us to those symbols in their structural place. Even so, talking to would-be or beginning writers, I find many of them working under the general assumption that the writer, somehow, must begin with such a synopsis (whether written down or no) and/or such an analysis.

This, for what it's worth, has not been my experience. At the beginning of a story, I am likely to have one or more images in my mind, some clearer than others (like the strip of light up Janice's arm), which, when I examine them, suggest relations to one another. Using the story process — envisioning and notating, envisioning and notating — I try to move from one of these images to the next, lighting and focusing, step by step, on the dark areas between. As I move along, other areas well ahead in the tale will suddenly come vaguely into light. When I actually reach the writing of them, I use the story process to bring them into sharper focus still.

As likely as not, some of the initial images will suggest obvious synopses of the material between (one image of a man on his knees before a safe; another of the same man fleeing across a rooftop while gunshots ring out behind; a third of the same man, marched between two policemen into a van) that the story process, when finished, will turn out to have followed pretty closely. But it is the process, not the synopsis, that produces the story. The synopsis is merely a guide.

Writers are always grappling with two problems: they must make the story interesting (to themselves, if no one else), yet keep it believable (because, somehow, when it ceases to be believable on some level, it ceases to be interesting).

Keeping things interesting seems to be primarily the province of the conscious mind (which, from the literature available, we know far less about than the unconscious), while believability is something that is supplied, in the images it throws up into the mind's theater, primarily by the unconscious. One thing we know about the unconscious is that it contains an incredibly complete "reality model," against which we are comparing our daily experiences moment to moment, every moment. This model lets us know that the thing over there is a garbage can while the thing over there is a gardenia bush, without our having to repeat the learning process of sticking our nose in them each time we pass. It also tells us that, though the thing over there *looks* like a gardenia bush, from a certain regularity in the leaves, an evenness in its coloring, and the tiny mold lines along the stem, it is really a plastic model of a gardenia bush and, should we sniff it, will not smell at all. The story process puts us closer to the material stored in our reality model than anything else we do besides dream. This material is what yielded up the splitting door jamb, the strip of light, the mattress ticking. This model is highly syncretic: reality is always presenting us with new experiences that are combinations of old ones. Therefore, even if we want to describe some Horatian impossibility "with the body of a lion and the head of an eagle," our model will give us, as we stare at the back of the creature's neck, the tawny hairs over the muscled shoulders, in which nestle the first mottled, orange-edge pin-feathers. Come to it honestly, and it will never lie: search as you want, it will not yield you the height of *pi*, the smell of the number seven, the sound of green, nor, heft hard as you can in the palm of your mind, the weight of the note D-flat. (This is not to suggest that such mysterious marvels aren't the province of fiction, especially science fiction; only that they are mysterious and marvelous constructions of the equally mysterious and marvelous *conscious* mind. That is where you must go to find out about *them*.)

When writers get (from readers or from themselves) criticism in the form "The story would be more believable if such and such happened" or "The story would be more interesting if such and such ... " *and* they agree to make use of the criticism, they must translate it: "Is there any point in the story process I can go back to, and, by examining my visualization more closely, catch something I missed before, which, when I notate it, will move the visualization/notation process forward again in this new way?" In other words, can the writers convince themselves that on some ideal level the story actually *did* happen (as opposed to "should have happened") in the new way, and that it was their inaccuracy as a story-process practitioner that got it going on the wrong track at some given point? If you don't do this, the corrections are going to clunk a bit and leave a patch-as-patch-can feel with the reader.

Writers work with the story process in different ways. Some writers like to work through a short story at a single, intense sitting, to interrupt as little as possible the energy that propels the process along, to keep the imagined visualization clearly and constantly in mind.

Other writers must pause, pace, and sometimes spend days between each few phrases, abandoning and returning to the visualization a dozen times a page. I think this is done as a sort of test, to make sure only the strongest and most vitally clear elements—the ones that cling tenaciously to the underside of memory—are retained.

Masterpieces have been written with both methods. Both methods have produced drivel.

In a very real way, one writes a story to find out what happens in it. Before it is written it sits in the mind like a piece of overheard gossip or a bit of intriguing tattle. The story process is like taking up such a piece of gossip, hunting down the people actually involved, questioning them, finding out what really occurred, and visiting pertinent locations. As with gossip, you can't be too surprised if important things turn up that were left out of the first-heard version entirely; or if points initially made much of turn out to have been distorted, or simply not to have happened at all.

Among those stories that strike us as perfectly plotted, with those astonishing endings both a complete surprise and a total satisfaction, it is amazing how many of their writers will confess that the marvelous resolution was as much a surprise for them as it was for the reader, coming, in imagination and through the story process, only a page or a paragraph or a word before its actual notation.

On the other hand, those stories that make us say, "Well, that's clever, *I suppose* ... ," but with a certain dissatisfied frown (the dissatisfaction itself, impossible to analyze), are often those stories worked out carefully in advance to be, precisely, clever.

One reason it is so hard to discuss the story process, even with introspection, is that it is something of a self-destruct process as well. The notation changes the imagination; it also distorts the writer's memory of the story's creation. The new, intensified visualization (which, depending on the success of the story process, and sometimes in spite of it, may or may not have anything to do with the reader's concept of the story) comes to replace the memory of the story process itself.

Writers cannot make any wholly objective statement on what they were trying to do, or even how they did it, because—as the only residue of the story process the reader has is the writer's words on the page—the only residue of the story process in the writer's mind is the clarified vision, which like the "plot" synopsis, is not the story, but the story's result.

New York City
1972

SAMUEL R. DELANY's science fiction and fantasy tales are available in *Aye and Gomorrah and Other Stories*. His collection *Atlantis: Three Tales* and *Phallos* are experimental fiction. His novels include science fiction such as the Nebula Award-winning *Babel-17* and *The Einstein Intersection*, as well as *Nova* (now in a Library of America anthology) and *Dhalgren*. His four-volume series Return to Nevèrÿon is sword-and-sorcery. Most recently, he has written the SF novel *Through the Valley of the Nest of Spiders*. His 2007 novel *Dark Reflections* won the Stonewall Book Award. Other novels include *Equinox*, *Hogg*, and *The Mad Man*. Delany was the subject of a 2007 documentary, *The Polymath*, by Fred Barney Taylor, and he has written a popular creative writing textbook, *About Writing*. He is the author of the widely taught *Times Square Red/Times Square Blue*, and his book-length autobiographical essay, *The Motion of Light in Water*, won a Hugo Award in 1989. As e-books, paperbacks, or audiobooks, his works are available through his website at www.samueldelany.com.

Some Thoughts on Exposition

TOBIAS S. BUCKELL

Science fiction, fantasy, historical fiction, or other fiction that deals with subject matter very unfamiliar to the reader has to accomplish two goals at the same time: educating the reader very quickly, while also entertaining them.

Set a novel in a country unfamiliar to the reader, in an odd line of work, or in a time period other than our own, and everything is different on a basic level: from what the people eat and why, to when they get up, to what their body language is. In order to not leave your reader completely confused, you will have to give them all the information they need in order to understand.

This *lump* of information is often a long paragraph or two describing something that the reader needs to know for the story to continue. But when you do that, it's like hitting pause on a show as the narrator steps forward and delivers the information. Or pausing and having a character explain to the viewers what's going on. It slows down the pace of the story, and for some readers, it breaks the fourth wall: it makes them aware that the author is clueing them in.

But if exposition is done well, a reader need never notice it.

Here are five ways I think about delivering expository information:

Flashback. This is a passage set in the foreground story's chronological past that delivers information about character interactions or experiences, or about other settings, that is necessary for the story to continue. You can slip into flashback as a character thinks about it, then dramatize it in the same way you've done the rest of the story up to that point. Or you can jump back in time at the start of a new section or chapter.

POSITIVES: Done well, a flashback increases understanding of what is going on and amps up tension.

NEGATIVES: It brings the foreground story to a screeching halt. It starts a new story. It stops the momentum.

Dialogue exposition. This is where a character with the requisite knowledge relays it to another character. If you've read Harry Potter, Rowling uses other characters, students and teachers at Hogwarts, to convey information to Harry that he doesn't have when arriving. But it's also, at the same time, educating the reader. And it's why many books have school-like settings and mentors who bring readers and characters up to speed on how the world works.

POSITIVES: You can use dialogue exposition to demonstrate how characters interact while also relaying needed information. Two princes arguing about the social situation of a land can clue the reader in to the history of your made-up country and also show that one of them thinks the countryside is fine, while the other thinks the peasants are about to revolt, thus allowing you to show something about each character.

NEGATIVES: The downside is that new writers often slip into having characters lecture other characters about information they wouldn't lecture about in real life. For example, I would never get into my car and turn to my wife and say "this *car* has an internal combustion system that drives a crankshaft, which, while spinning, sets the wheels in motion, thus driving us forward." (For examples of badly delivered dialogue exposition used for humor, check out the movie *The Lost Skeleton of Cadavra*, which I often use in lectures to sink this point home.) A sign of badly done dialogue exposition is the phrase 'as you know.' In science fiction, we call such weak dialogue exposition *As you know, Bob*.

Narrator exposition. This is quite common. Sometimes in fiction you'll see sentences like this: *Tom looked at the car. It was an old internal combustion device, the explosions inside driving a crankshaft, which spun and produced power to the wheels.*

The narrator is the space where the writer is putting in words that aren't in the characters' heads or in their dialogue. In a lot of popular fiction, the narrators keep their heads down, and are mostly invisible, which is why a sentence suddenly explaining an engine sticks out. This is the classic *infodump*, or simply *exposition*.

Classic infodumping is not a problem if your style favors the narrative voice being a part of the story's character. For examples, humorous asides and infodumps are a part of Terry Pratchett's work, and Neal Stephenson's obsession with pieces of interesting backstory and history make his infodumps fascinating to his readers, as they're reading for just that sort of thing.

POSITIVES: Narrator exposition gives the reader information the author thinks they need.

NEGATIVES: It stands out, it slows things down, and it can be perceived as clunky. But sometimes you just can't figure out another way to do it, so you just have to drop it in.

Exposition through a character's internal voice. Think of every hard-boiled detective novel, and you'll get what I'm talking about. A grim private investigator looks at a woman and thinks, *She'd always gotten what she wanted: she was like a pit bull when she wanted something, those lovely eyes locking into you and grabbing a hold and never letting go until you've said yes. That's how she'd gotten the divorce papers from me ...*

With this type of exposition, you're doing something similar to a narrative infodump, but through the character's voice. It tends to go down smoother, because you're not *just* expositing, but also developing character. In general, expositing *plus* doing something else works best.

POSITIVES: You get to do two things at the same time, reveal character and voice, while also giving the reader needed information. Done well, it's invisible and smooth.

NEGATIVES: Your character ends up stopping the story to deliver a monologue at the reader that breaks the suspension of disbelief.

Interacting with the information. In some science fiction circles Robert Heinlein is famous for writing "the door dilated," which reveals that the setting is in the future, and that doors work differently, and doing it all without having to club you over the head.

Instead of explaining how a rocket works, just have your character get into one and be launched: that will take the reader through the experience. Watching the character go and bang on a hyperdrive that isn't working and have pieces break lets readers see the character physically interacting and working with the information you need to give them.

POSITIVES: Whenever you can get a character to directly interact with the environment it helps make the setting feel real to the reader.

NEGATIVES: Get too lost in showing every little thing and the story loses balance and can take too long to move on for the reader. Just like a painter has to suggest a curve of a body with a single brush stroke, a writer has to carefully choose what they show.

The key to making exposition work is not depending on any single one of these techniques, but in incorporating all of these tricks throughout a story and scattering them evenly in between elements of dialogue, action, plot, and description to create what some people call *marbling*. Even if you have to use just a straight chunk of information, keeping it to a sentence or two, buried inside of something else interesting, works best.

When I was starting as a writer, I would take a published story in a magazine with a highlighter and mark all the different ways in which expository information was delivered with different colors. Another good exercise was to write out a piece of information in a lump, then write three scenes, trying to slip the information into them using any of the above methods. Seeing which one read better helped me figure out which method I liked best in each instance.

Many writers try to eliminate as much exposition as they can in the fear that they need to focus on showing and not telling. It's true that we need to dramatize as much of the story as we can, but if we don't keep the reader informed on what they need to know for the dramatized bits to make sense, we fail our job as storytellers. Like anything in life, it's a matter of balance. A well-marbled manuscript will draw your reader through.

Called "violent, poetic and compulsively readable" by *Maclean's*, science fiction author **TOBIAS S. BUCKELL** is a *New York Times* Bestselling writer and World Fantasy Award winner born in the Caribbean. He grew up in Grenada and spent time in the British and US Virgin Islands, and the islands he lived on influence much of his work. His Xenowealth series begins with *Crystal Rain*. Along with other stand-alone novels and his almost one hundred stories, his works have been translated into nineteen different languages. He has been nominated for awards like the Hugo, Nebula, World Fantasy, and the Astounding Award for Best New Science Fiction Author. His latest novel is *The Tangled Lands*, written with Paolo Bacigalupi, which the *Washington Post* said is "a rich and haunting novel that explores a world where magic is forbidden."

He currently lives in Bluffton, Ohio, with his wife, and two daughters. He can be found online at TobiasBuckell.com and is also an instructor at the Stonecoast MFA in Creative Writing program.

The Devil Is in the Details

CONNIE WILLIS

> "In all my experience along the dirtiest ways of the dirty world, I have never met with such a thing as a trifle yet."
>
> —WILKIE COLLINS

Writers spend most of their time focusing on the big stuff—plot, characters, dialogue, scene construction—and those are certainly important. But in the end, it all comes down to the details, to what Jane Austen called "the minute particulars." These "particulars" are the building blocks from which stories are constructed. They're what make the story palpable, believable, and memorable—and, if we're lucky, what capture the meaning of the story and convey it to the reader.

One of the main things details do is set the scene for the story. They're what convince us we're in an enchanted forest or a Brooklyn tenement or a spaceship lying just off the rings of Saturn rather than sitting at home reading a book.

What do you think of when someone mentions Sherlock Holmes? Lamplighters, fog, deerstalker hats, and horse-drawn hansom cabs clip-clopping along a cobblestone street.

Mention Frank Herbert's *Dune*, and we think of deserts, sandworms, black-shrouded nuns, and eyes blue with spice.

Mention Raymond Chandler's mysteries and we see fedoras, palm trees, seedy Los Angeles bars, and a gun and a bottle of rye in a desk drawer.

Actually, that's not quite accurate. What we see—or think we see—is an entire landscape: 1940s Los Angeles, the planet Arrakis, turn-of-the-century London. But that landscape exists only in our imaginations. It's actually been conjured up out of a few well-chosen details—details which function like a magician's props to create an elaborate illusion.

But they can't be just any details. They have to be specific and vivid. And evocative. Sometimes that means exotic—a glass slipper, a diamond stolen from the forehead of a Hindu idol, a

Maltese falcon—but they don't necessarily have to be. Evocative details can also be ordinary: an umbrella or a pair of candlesticks or the green light at the end of a boat dock.

Or a flyswatter. In the movie *1776*, one of the most expressive details is John Hancock's flyswatter. It functions by turns as a gavel, an exclamation point, a weapon, and a reminder of the heat and insects that plagued the writers of the Declaration of Independence.

Details also have to engage the senses. "My task," Joseph Conrad said, "... is, by the power of the written word, to make you hear, to make you feel—it is, before all, to make you see," and that's done with details: the wail of a train whistle, the scent of lilacs, the feel of a sudden gust of icy wind, the taste of a hot dog with mustard.

But there's a catch: the details you use have to be accurate. This applies not only to historical and scientific details, but to everyday things, to what time of year peonies bloom and what direction streets run. It's essential that you get things right. As Friedrich Nietzsche said, "The devil is in the details."

He's right. Incorrect details can kill a story. Everyone's read a story with an error in it—the outlaw on the run from the sheriff's posse who hides out in the mountains of Western Kansas, the sophomore at Harvard who gets hauled into the principal's office, the Roman senator who pulls out a pocket watch. Or a smart phone. In my early days I wrote a story set in midtown Manhattan where my heroine got distracted while driving and hit a tree. (It must have been the one from *A Tree Grows in Brooklyn* since otherwise there's not a tree in sight.)

Incorrect details like that break the spell the writer is trying to cast and kick the reader right out of the story. And I'm not just talking about details that are important to the story. It can be any detail that does it, no matter how tiny or irrelevant. I've gotten irate letters from readers about my saying the people in *Topper* were drinking martinis rather than pink ladies or that the Candyland game had a molasses swamp card. ("It has a Molasses Swamp," the reader wrote indignantly, "but not a Molasses Swamp card!")

No detail is too small to potentially ruin the reading experience. Which means it's the writer's duty to get everything right, from dates to fashions to the name of that little doohickey on the airplane dashboard that tells you whether you're maintaining your flight level (the vertical speed indicator).

This means doing lots of research (including double-checking those facts you think you already know), but it's as essential as the details themselves.

Finally, there are details which resonate with meaning and create indelible images that stay with the reader. Take *The Grapes of Wrath*, John Steinbeck's novel about displaced Oklahoma farmers during the Dust Bowl. In it, there's a description of a turtle who's been knocked on his back while trying to cross a highway. He struggles hopelessly to right himself amid the traffic whizzing by and threatening to hit him at any second.

It's a vivid detail—and it's a lot more. It's a perfect metaphor for the poor displaced Oklahoma farmer, upended by circumstances and struggling to get back on his feet against impossible odds.

Steinbeck's turtle is a perfect example of what's called a "telling detail," a detail that functions as a powerful symbol in the story. The antique gilded crystal bowl in Henry James's *The Golden Bowl* is another example, and so is the packet of postcards in E. M. Forster's *A Room with a View*. Lucy Honeychurch buys the packet of postcards of views of Florence in the Plaza like any tourist, but when they're covered with the blood of a man who's killed in a fight right in front of her, they become a symbol for the world's violent realities that are suddenly splashed across her innocent holiday—and across her consciousness.

Telling details can symbolize a feeling or an idea in a story, or they can even, in certain instances, capture the essence of the story. When I was writing *Lincoln's Dreams*, a novel about the Civil War, I went to Fredericksburg. I needed to check on several details—what the public library looked like (it was in an old brick school building) and how big the battlefield was (impossibly tiny) and what it looked like.

When I toured the battlefield, I noticed a bunch of small round cement markers with numbers on them—59-2 and 83-4 and 124-6. I assumed they indicated where soldiers had fallen, but when I asked the park ranger about them, he told me they were grave markers. "The first figure is the registry number of the grave," he said, "and the second is the number of bodies buried under it."

Oh, my God! 59-2, 85-4, 124-6, and nearly all of them unidentified. I had read thousands of pages of details about battles and casualties and deaths, but none of them brought home the horror and tragedy of the Civil War, of young boys killed and flung together into nameless graves with no one ever knowing what happened to them, like those humble markers. They crystallized the theme of the book for me and became its heart.

This is what Vladimir Nabokov was talking about when he described the "secret nerves" of the story, "the secret points, the subliminal coordinates." Those "secret nerves" can be anything. For Proust's *Remembrance of Things Past*, it was a small, shell-shaped cookie, the madeleine. For Tolstoy's *Anna Karenina*, it was "a bare exquisite aristocratic elbow." For Nabokov's *Lolita*, it was a beautiful butterfly pinned to a board. Whatever it is, it reverberates with meaning for the writer and the reader, sending chills up their spines and capturing the essence of the story.

All of these different kinds of minute particulars—the telling details, the secret nerves, the details which set the scene and provide verisimilitude—are crucial to good writing. They're just as important as plot and character and deserve just as much attention from the writer.

The devil may be in the details, but what Ludwig Mies van der Rohe said is closer to the truth. One of the most important architects of the twentieth century, he knew everything there was to know about building skyscrapers, and it applies to writing, too. "God is in the details," he said. Keep that in mind when building your next story.

Grand Master of Science Fiction **CONNIE WILLIS** is the author of Nebula and Hugo Award-winning novels about a gaggle of time-travelling Oxford historians—*Doomsday Book*, *To Say Nothing of the Dog*, *Blackout*, and *All Clear*—as well as *Passage*, *Crosstalk*, the soon-to-be-published *The Road to Roswell*, and numerous short stories, the writing of all of which have firmly convinced her that the devil is, indeed, in the details. So here are a couple more: Willis has an English bulldog named Bunter (after Lord Peter Wimsey's butler) and two cats who look exactly alike named Claudia and Jenny (after Connie's favorite BBC show *Primeval*). I repeat, they look EXACTLY alike.

Coincidentally ...

STEPHEN GRAHAM JONES

There aren't many ironclad rules in fiction writing. There are techniques and tricks and devices that seem to work more often than not, that can *feel* like rules, but then some hotshot comes along and blasts that all to — as Harlan Ellison might say — flinders. Or maybe a writer who doesn't know all of these supposedly bulletproof rules tells their story in a completely unexpected, never-been-done way that no one would ever suggest ... and it all works out fine, and the rest of us are just playing catch-up. Or some Elmore Leonard type will tell us never to open a novel talking about the weather, then go on to do exactly that over and over, and it doesn't break the world.

Talking or not talking about the weather could just come down to taste, though. As for rules that seem less subjective ... how about the injunction against switching from first to third person capriciously? For me, this one's very nearly ironclad. At least until my novel *Mongrels*, which is first person intercut with sections of third — the only way I could make work what I needed to work. My *The Only Good Indians* breaks this injunction even more egregiously, toggling from third person to second *without* section breaks, which was the only way I could make happen what I thought needed to happen.

Or ... another rule, another rule. Yeah: Stay in a single tense, please? But there's some beautiful amazing stories out there that don't (Mona Simpson's "Lawns"). I've even read a story that's all in that always warned-against passive voice (Elisabeth Sheffield's "Sugar Smacks"), and that story slays, could only be told as well as it is with precisely all these passive constructions.

So, rules don't exactly always rule. Theory's great, but feet-on-the-ground — or, on the page, anyway — often make tactics necessary that you'd never even considered considering.

Then of course there's our own personal rules we each develop to get across the page, yes? These tend to be so deeply ingrained that they feel less like rules, more like a system of narrative ethics. A couple of mine:

- Start flashy, with some sort of bang.
- Don't hang around to clean up the Shire.

However, just because these feel so right to me doesn't make them ironclad. Exceptions abound, probably even in stuff I've published — maybe whatever I write next does that *The Name of the Rose* slowdown for the first hundred pages, and then drags the end way past the actual end, like when you're on the phone saying bye to someone you don't really want off the line.

Still and all, though, there is one so-called rule where there doesn't seem to be any wiggle room:

Coincidence only enables, it never solves.

Which — I should probably disentangle coincidence from irony, right fast. Coincidence is arbitrary, random, and it doesn't suggest some providential path or greater system or intention. The hard and fast definition of "coincidence" is that it's a concurrence of events with no causal connection. In story terms, *coincidence* is that Alice happens to look up at the exact time that very late rabbit is hopping past. And then everything else happens *because* of that coincidence.

Irony, in story terms ... we all know *The Twilight Zone*, don't we? In "Time Enough at Last," the protagonist in this postapocalyptic world is thrilled he can finally read all the books he wants! Except — get that sad slide whistle ready — his glasses, which he needs to make this dream come true, are now broken. Why? Because the universe has a sense of humor, and nothing's funnier to it than a heaping dose of poetic justice. It's what cautionary tales need to get the job done. Or, to go to the page for some irony, O. Henry's "The Gift of the Magi," where a husband and wife each want to surprise each other with the perfect gift, but in order to buy that gift they have to sell what's most dear to them: her hair; his pocket watch. Only, when they trade gifts, it turns out the husband's bought his wife a set of nice combs for the hair she no longer has, and the wife's bought her husband a nice fob for that watch he sold.

Irony has its use, definitely, and it's not showing any signs of fatigue. But it's not coincidence. Coincidence is that "concurrence of events with no causal connection." It's random, it's arbitrary, and it's an integral part of the beginning of most stories.

Here's how it *should* work: a tornado touches down *here*, not *there*, so it scoops up *this* house, not any of the rest of the houses in Kansas, and it sets that house down ... on the Wicked Witch of the West, in some place called Oz. Despite the fact that Dorothy here turns out to be the chosen one, still, that tornado (the portal of this portal fantasy) snatching the house instead of the barn, that's a concurrence of events with no causal connection. And *because* of this coincidence, the rest of the story happens. Or, or ... Neil Gaiman's *The Graveyard Book*, say: if there's not a graveyard up the hill for this toddler to toddle up into, then the rest of the story doesn't happen. Coincidences *enable*. Random intersections at the front of stories aren't just acceptable, I think they might even be necessary.

They're much harder to accept at the end, though.

Karma being what it is, I probably shouldn't trundle anyone's work in as an example of how *not* to do it, so play-pretend with me for a bit, here: an FBI profiler and a serial killer have been doing their cat-and-mouse thing across the city for three- or four-hundred pages, and at the end of this long and involved chase, which has involved all the necessary close calls and near misses we could ask for, the serial killer is at the top of a slide with her pistol leveled at the profiler, who's a few feet down the slide, having to hold on to keep from sluicing down to that kiddy pool way at the bottom. Monologue aside, this should be the end of story, right? Except ... then the water that keeps this slide slick surges on as it must every minute or two, the killer loses her balance *and* the pistol, and falls right down into the profiler's waiting handcuffs — end of story.

Doesn't feel good, does it? It's "happy," sure, but it's not *earned*. This profiler didn't have to use their wits or muscles or water-park experience to win the day. It's as if Scarecrow's just blown a fear-gas dart right at Batman's neck, and a random pigeon flies between at just the right/wrong moment, is now going to have a scary afternoon. What we *prefer* is for Batman's Spidey-sense to kick on at the last moment, so he can limber up his cannister of anti-dart spray.

To say it differently, if the profiler "wins" in this lucky, random, unearned way, then all their strife and toil up to this point has now become meaningless. Anyone in the Bureau could have been there when that slide's water surged on. A teenage *lifeguard* could have been and it would have been same result, just, with make-do handcuffs. What a coincidence at the end of a story does is make all the story *before* this point no longer matter. The profiler could just as well have spent the first three- or four-hundred pages organizing their desk and filing their files, then, at the appointed time, leaned up the wet stairs of a certain water slide, stopped the most heinous serial killer since the last one.

Instant hero.

Well, "instant hero" in a story that didn't pay out on your investment of time and energy, emotion and hope. But we all prefer the Batman kind of hero instead, don't we? The kind who has to work and struggle for each small victory.

This isn't at all to say coincidence is necessarily bad, though. Just, its *placement* is what can be terrible. At the end, coincidence is an eraser. At the beginning, it's a doorway, doesn't feel random at all, but the kind of fortunate that doesn't have to be earned.

The reader will accept nearly any coincidence at the beginning of a story.

At the end, though? If there's a coincidence at the end that saves the day, then the real coincidence will be that reader ever accidentally picking up one of your stories again.

STEPHEN GRAHAM JONES is the author of twenty-five or so novels and collections, and there's some novellas and comic books in there as well. Stephen's been an NEA recipient, has won the Texas Institute of Letters Award for Fiction, the Independent Publishers Award for Multicultural Fiction, a Bram Stoker Award, four This Is Horror Awards, and he's been a finalist for the Shirley Jackson Award and the World Fantasy Award. He's also made Bloody Disgusting's Top Ten Horror Novels, and is the guy who wrote *Mongrels* and *The Only Good Indians*. Stephen lives in Boulder, Colorado.

Channeling Voices

ANDY DUNCAN

My first fiction-writing teacher was the late William Price Fox, writer in residence at the University of South Carolina when I was an undergraduate. He told us once about a run-in with a copy editor over the first sentence of one of his stories:

> Brother, have you ever rode the Southern from Atlanta to Columbia?

Our magazine's readers are in big coastal towns, the editor argued, and won't know where these places are. (As if *Southern* weren't a hint.) The editor's proposed rewrite was this:

> Brother, have you ever rode the Southern from Atlanta, Georgia, to Columbia, South Carolina?

All the students in the room groaned. We were novice writers at best, but we instantly grasped that the rewrite would ruin the opening. Fox's original sentence had the rhythm of a forward-moving train, whereas the rewrite forced the train off the tracks to smash into a heap at the bottom of a ravine.

Moreover, we knew enough about the story's narrator, from our brief acquaintance of only eleven words, to understand that he would never see the need to clarify which states he was talking about, any more than he would see the need to clarify that the Southern was a railroad and not an airline.

While it's irrelevant to the editor's objection, and therefore to Fox's point in telling us the anecdote, I just realized—as I typed the paragraph above—something else we all instinctively understood from the story's first sentence: that the narrator should be read as male.

This is established by the opening word, the salutation "Brother"—both chummy and conspiratorial, as in, "You and I are men of the world, and can speak frankly among ourselves, and therefore I now will tell you something that you, too, are qualified to understand."

Yes, in the South of my childhood, women sometimes used "Brother" as a substitute name for a male sibling, but if our narrator were addressing a sibling, Brother's travel history would be known already, and there would be no need to ask about it.

In fact, our narrator is not addressing someone he knows well. He's addressing an acquaintance, perhaps even someone he just met, just fell into conversation with, invited or uninvited —perhaps even the stranger who happens to be sitting next to him on a train.

That is a lot of information to convey in eleven words! The rhythm bears meaning as a railroad car bears freight, but the sentence's cargo of words makes a contribution, too.

Bill Fox's anecdote, I now realize, was my first lesson in *voice*, in the sound and sense of the words working in unison. I think of it like the music and lyrics that together comprise a song. When voice is present—in other words, when sound and sense work together—the effect is not only unmistakable, compelling, resonant; it also renders the passage vastly more informative than it otherwise would have been. Multiple information streams are suddenly reaching us.

Voice is hard to talk about, even for veteran writers—though we sure do recognize it when we read it or write it—and when we make the effort, we often err in emphasizing sound over sense, or to the exclusion of sense. For one thing, that unnecessarily privileges hearing, though both *voice* and *sound*, as used here, are textual effects independent of the ears. Even more importantly, voice is nothing if it is not equally the sound and the sense, enmeshed and impossible to separate ... as when a firefighter barks an order, or a loved one has a confidence to share.

Through the years, fans have told me, "As I read your stories, I can hear your voice in my head." I don't think they mean my speaking/reading voice, but my voice *on the page*—which I work harder at, probably, than any other aspect of my writing, in both fiction and nonfiction.

And in most pieces, I'm actually trying to convey *voices*, plural —multiple speakers, multiple perspectives—which may or may not reflect my own speaking voice, my own perspectives. After all, I have never been a Black blues musician in the Depression era, or a medieval Vatican henchman, or a Cold War-era Soviet rocket engineer, or a lesbian geocacher, or Harry Houdini, all of whom I've attempted to convey convincingly and sympathetically in my stories. (See *Writing the Other: A Practical Approach* by Nisi Shawl and Cynthia Ward, from Aqueduct Press, for brilliant guidance here.)

My basic training in voice came long before I got serious about writing fiction. In my four years as a full-time newspaper reporter in North Carolina, my daily duties involved interviewing multiple people—usually in person, in their homes or workplaces—and writing down everything they said, exactly as they said it, then trying to reproduce that experience for the readers in a way that truthfully conveyed who these people were.

I spent hours with a barbecue cook, a schoolteacher on a coastal island, an exiled Chilean dissident, a professional harpist, a retiree who had been the first Black woman judge in North Carolina, a Methodist pastor turned queer activist, a former State Department spokesman, a man obsessed with Styrofoam, a roadside vendor of black-velvet paintings, a cigarette-factory worker who had led an armed occupation at Columbia University in 1968, and Waylon Jennings. I walked the beat with cops, crawled through caves with spelunkers, went aloft with airship captains, attended school board meetings and Grateful Dead concerts and murder trials and Renaissance fairs.

I quickly learned that what people said often was less interesting than how they said it. Here, for example, is a bit of my attempt to convey how Polly Yow, a choral director at a rural high school, expressed herself.

> "I never have understood why they built me such a big office," she says, slapping her desk with a stack of freshman exams. "I bet every one of those boys failed this test. I can't wait to grade 'em. Keith, honey, just leave that till tomorrow. ... This is the hardest group I've ever seen to get under my thumb," Yow says, holding up a crooked thumb for emphasis. "They're freshmen, and they're

in high school, and they think they know everything. I told 'em, 'If some of you were as big as you think you are you'd be a giant.' Don't you *take* my picture smoking that cigarette and put it in the paper."

Lifelong habits were acquired during this time. To this day, I habitually eavesdrop on strangers and, on the spot or immediately afterward, write down what they say. For example, in O'Hare Airport in June 2005, on my way to Seattle to teach at Clarion West, I was entertained by several card-playing kids. At one point, the leader's mom interrupted.

BOY: All I have are crap cards!
MOM: We'll have no language like that. Go with your father to look for sandwiches.
BOY: I'm not hungry.
MOM: You will be. It's a four-hour flight.
BOY: We just had lunch.
MOM: We did not have lunch. We had Taco Bell. Go with your father.
BOY: No.
MOM: You would not be happy if I took your Game Boy away for the whole four-hour flight.
BOY: I'd break into your purse.
MOM: No you wouldn't, because I'd catch you.
(Pause.)
BOY: You'll have to sleep *sometime*.

Other lifelong habits: I collect glossaries — of regional speech, criminal speech, historical speech. No matter what I'm reading, I make note of every unfamiliar word, phrase and cultural reference, and look it up afterward. Then I plow as many of these back into my stories as possible.

"Beluthahatchie" began with a set of words and phrases that I was determined to string together, somehow, into a coherent voice, including the place name that became the title, which I learned from Zora Neale Hurston. "Close Encounters," on the other hand, was a complete first draft when I decided its voice wasn't Ozark enough, so I went back and translated dozens of passages into words and phrases from a glossary compiled by Vance Randolph. (Thanks again to my bookseller friend Mark Wingenfeld, for sending me that book in the first place.)

By "words and phrases," remember, I mean "sounds and senses."

I also sometimes get into the voice of a character or a narrator by "casting" people whose voices I know well (actors or non-actors, living or dead), and taking dictation as those people speak in my head.

To recap, the *voice* of a piece of fiction—which, to me, means both sound and sense, working in unison—is determined by multiple factors, a few of which include:

- sentence length
- sentence complexity
- sentence rhythm
- repetition (words, phrases, vowels, consonants)
- formality/informality of language
- familiarity/unfamiliarity of language (the unfamiliar including slang, archaisms, neologisms, technical terms, jargon, regionalisms, dialect, individual character quirks, etc.)
- markers of time and/or place (including imagined/invented times and places)
- attitude (overt or implied)
- characterization (Whose words *are* these?)
- context (What is the *occasion* of these words?)

Does any of this help? I wonder. Voice in fiction, I hope to convey, is both insanely complicated and infinitely rewarding.

If I realize that I have hit on the right voice, then I know I'm onto something—even if I have to go back and rewrite the plot, rewrite the structure, rewrite the characters, just to fit the voice. If the voice is good, the story is good.

When Christian Coleman interviewed me for *Lightspeed* in 2018, I realized something about my Small Beer Press collection,

An Agent of Utopia, that pleased me very much. The first sentence of the first story in the book, on page 1, is this:

> To the Prince and Tranibors of our good land, and the offices of the Syphogrants below, and all those families thereof, greetings, from your poor servant in far Albion.

The last sentence of the last story in the book, on page 276, is this:

> "Hey, Mr. Nelson? Is this your dog?"

Reading the first and last sentences of every book, every novel, every story, will teach you a lot about voice. What I told Christian, though, was: "Those two sentences—that's my career, right there."

ANDY DUNCAN attended Clarion West 1994, returned to teach in 2005 and 2015, and is scheduled to teach Week One in 2021. His short-fiction honors include a Nebula Award, a Theodore Sturgeon Memorial Award, and three World Fantasy Awards. His third collection, *An Agent of Utopia: New and Selected Stories*, was published by Small Beer Press in 2018, and Andy reads nine of its stories on the audio edition, from Recorded Books. A South Carolina native, he is a professor of writing at Frostburg State University in the mountains of western Maryland, where he lives with his wife, Sydney.

Status

HELEN MARSHALL

Quarter to ten in the morning on a Saturday. A *Saturday*.

I'm sweating in my silk blouse and comfortable navy slacks, jogging through the University of Queensland's Great Court (sandstone pillars in swirls of gold and periwinkle, faux-Oxbridge gargoyles leering down). Humidity thick as fog. My heels are an inch higher than I'd like. I don't know where I'm going, only that my class—Writing the Novel—is scheduled to kick off any minute and I seem to be locked out.

So are the students.

The gaggle observes me with interest, the youngest with their stickered laptops and color-coordinated notebooks murmuring to each other with raised eyebrows. The sexagenarians in the group are uniformly frowning. They think I'm hopeless—but I'm not. Really. I'd scoped the route to the classroom the week before—but that had been during working hours. On weekends the security protocols must be different. Damn.

Sighing, I flash a conspiratorial smile at Graci, the only one among them I recognize: round-faced with thick, purple-framed glasses. *Isn't this an adventure?* She grins and whispers to her friend, a slender woman with stylish blonde hair who taps her pen against her notebook.

Not a good beginning.

It takes a frantic search to find the right room: a maze of corridors, a fruitless elevator journey to the fourth floor only to realize, yes, that door is locked as well.

But then here we are, ready to begin.

The experience of teaching creative writing calls to my mind the writings of the theater expert Keith Johnstone, whom I first encountered as an undergraduate. To be honest, I was pretty lousy in those acting classes. Too self-conscious, too stuck in my own head.

But there was something in it that stayed with me over the years, guiding my approach both to writing scenes and surviving in the classroom. Johnstone understood humans—living, breathing, fighting, flirting, angry, obsequious, passionate humans—in a way that eluded me. See, I was a watcher. Shy in groups, never the first to speak—but with eyes wide open. What was I taking in exactly? Even I couldn't have told you: only that the cut-and-thrust of a glance and a well-placed word seemed to me as dramatic as a fencing match. I remember in Oxford hearing a tutor exclaim, "That's all so *interesting*," in such a way that you knew someone was being flayed alive. (The English are experts at this sort of killing politeness.) The trick, Johnstone suggested in *Impro*, which laid out his theory, was realizing that at the heart of every human interaction was a play for status.

Imagine a CEO. Silk tie, expensive shoes, three-hundred-dollar haircut. Can you see him in your mind? Good. Now watch him as he strides into his conference room ... As a writer, what can you do to make him lose control?

Maybe he slips on a banana peel. Maybe he's got fresh paint stains on his trouser legs. Maybe Sharon from HR is waiting for him. Or his gorgeous ex-wife—with a gun.

Note what happens when he realizes something is different. How does his voice change? How much do his shoulders sag? What are his hands doing? Are they fidgeting or balling into white-knuckled fists? Does he stay and fight? Does he shrink? Does he crumble?

It isn't so different in the classroom.

As a teacher, you start with a certain authority, but it's marginal and liable to vanish as easily a soap bubble. So. I get to work laying out course texts, handouts, scratchpads for doodling. I don't make eye contact with the students. Not yet. They still need time to settle.

This is the first class I've taught at the University of Queensland, so I don't quite know what to expect from them. Where are their heads at? My previous students were mostly first-generation school-goers: warm and unpretentious, slow to speak up but quick to form friendships. This group strikes me as more wary.

Graci has taken a seat at the front of the room. She and her friend chat lightly to each other. No one else has bothered with them yet. The others have spread out at the desks into groups of four and five. As always, a few stragglers position themselves at tables by themselves — the watchers — only reluctantly packing up their things when I ask them to come closer. It's important in a creative writing classroom that everyone feels in it together.

But that takes work.

Writing students can be horribly hierarchical, worse than baboons or wolves. As I finish my prep, the jostling for dominance has already begun. Who has published? Who hasn't? Marwan pins his rejections to the wall with an old nail, just like Stephen King did when he was starting out. "Doesn't matter if they like it yet," he mutters half to himself. "They will."

Gladys, sitting across the table, grimaces. She's a retired English teacher and can't abide misused semicolons, which she circles in red pen. Old habits die hard. She's spent her life teaching fourteen-year-olds to read Shakespeare and has never shown her writing to anyone. I worry she'll be brittle and cantankerous, but I'll discover in her a surprising generosity that makes her much loved by her classmates.

Graci and her friend are both editors for a small literary magazine which they started three years ago. When someone makes this known, they find themselves suddenly the objects of intense fascination.

Johnstone frames status as the power difference in the relationship between two or more characters. We tend to think of status as fixed or inherent, a function of one's position, upbringing, clothing, physique, but he argues status is a constant performance and it's seldom stable. In the most interesting encounters, it swings up and down like a seesaw.

In one moment the CEO is in control of the boardroom: he holds the floor, he has no problem making eye contact with his subordinates. But then something happens ...

It is a doctor's office he is stepping into this time, not a board room. Then he hears the news: his son has been in a terrible accident. He feels as if he's been punched in the stomach. That same violation: grief.

The doctor is younger than him — blue-eyed and baby-faced — which makes it all somehow worse. There are tears in his eyes too, which doesn't make sense because the man doesn't know Jamie. He's never met him. Is this his first time delivering bad news or what? The CEO hates trainees of all stripes. Hates incompetence, any show of weakness. Shouldn't they have wheeled in the Chief of Staff for this? Don't they know who he goddamn is?

A deep breath steadies me.

I walk out from behind the lectern. A ripple of glances, then the spreading hush. This is the hardest part, I've learned. Waiting. Letting them make the decision to give you the room.

As you might guess, I'm not a natural public speaker. I remember out-of-body experiences in grade school, a breath away from tears, my tiny hands clutching my carefully prepared cue cards. I built my thoughts carefully like a child stacking blocks, and I hated putting them on display until I was absolutely ready.

Then at twenty-three, I stepped in front of an undergraduate class for the first time. No choice. I wanted to be a professor and I *had* to learn — somehow. Teaching a class isn't anything like writing an essay. It's a performance, an invitation, a developing relationship. It needs tact and courage and a sense of humor. But in that early attempt it was like someone had trapped me in a standing glass coffin. Frozen in fear, my arms jerked robotically. I knew I had to gesture. But when? How to punctuate without flailing? I flinched when the mousy first-row brunette raised her hand.

It's different now.

I've been teaching for close to ten years and I've learned to leave my water bottle at the far side of the room so I always have a reason to walk if I want one. My gaze moves in a zee-pattern, working my way to the front. I linger on the smiles, slip past the neutral thinking frowns.

Status interests us. As children it doesn't take much to pick up the basic schoolyard hierarchy. Who has power, who can be pushed around. *In* group and *out* group. Put five strangers in a room together and you'll see them sort it out soon enough. Aristotle said humans are social animals. Think of a wolf pack. We're all more comfortable when we know where we stand.

But we like to see others working it out. It interests us. The most boring scene comes to life when you play with the statuses of the characters. And you can do it with the lightest of touches. A gesture, a glance, a question.

Imagine this: The CEO calls his wife from the hospital. Deborah has no idea what has happened yet. She lives in another world, a world where the old reality still holds sway.

"When are you coming home?" she asks. Is she shrewish or plaintive? The CEO can't really tell anymore. Normally his secretary will answer these sorts of questions for him.

He could answer any number of ways. (This is a great exercise. Vary your responses. Character comes from specifics.)

"I don't know yet." Neutral, he thinks, but could she read in his voice that something is wrong? "When I'm good and ready!" He's tired now and his anger is irrational, aimed at the driver of the white Ford — still unknown — and not his wife of seventeen years.

The CEO knows he'll need her now. More than ever. She's stronger than he is, always has been. He can't survive this alone. "As soon as I can," he whispers: understated, apologetic but she can sense the shift in his voice. "All right, darling," she says, "when you can." He waits for something else but she's already hung up the phone.

It's difficult to find your natural status as a teacher.

I started with a strange mixture of hideous conceit and fraudulence. I'd been trained to spot faults but I still hadn't really experienced how very difficult it is to build something new myself. It made me paranoid and simultaneously eager to please. Now I'm a bit looser. I don't like to dominate if I can help it. Mostly this works. Not always.

We're two hours into the session, and Marwan looks disgruntled, but that's okay. I've told him that although I love writing more than *anything* in the world, I also hate it with the white-hot rage of a thousand suns. I will do nearly anything to *not write*. I will do the dishes, scrub the toilet, answer students' e-mails — *anything*. Because writing is hard and it almost always makes me feel like I'm failing.

Marwan doesn't wasn't to hear this.

Marwan wants to hear about book deals and film options and six-figure advances. He wants to know all those rejections nailed to his wall *mean* something and that this is only the tricky part at the beginning of the story he'll one day recite to a crowd of fans at the launch of his thirty-seventh bestseller.

Maybe at the end of the class he'll raise his hand and ask me, "So what would you do differently? You know, so I don't ..."

... *end up like you*, he means. Those who can't do, teach — right?

And a host of heads will perk up like little meerkats.

We're in the jungle now. This is the moment you can feel the seesaw moving. It can be grim and scary but also — I've learned — exhilarating. Because this is the real test of status. The high heels, the silk blouse, the accoutrements of my profession mean nothing if I can't hold my place. The students have to *trust* me. If they don't, they'll check out. Ignore feedback. Make mistakes they could avoid.

So how do I prove to him I'm worth listening to? I could point to my awards shelf and show him the blurbs I have from his heroes. (I'm high status, see? Or maybe I'm just Donald Trump bragging about my bigly words.) I could point out that fewer than a thousand writers in America make a living from writing. (I'm higher than those who have tried and failed, right?) Or I could take the Oxford route: cut down his writing, whip out my red pen, tell him his chances. It would shut him up ...

And shut him down.

His eyes would go stony and cold. Maybe he'd crumble. Maybe he'd fight me. Maybe he'd quit the class. Or maybe he'd think of the encounter as just one more rejection, one more gatekeeper who will rue the day when he's famous. Maybe.

But I want him in the class. I want him to listen. I want him to know—in the kindest way possible—that most of what he thinks he knows about writing probably isn't true. Which is why I'm here.

My job isn't to terrorize or dominate him. A writing career is just a game of snakes and ladders. Sometimes you're up, sometimes you're down. Really, I'm just a guide—one guide among the many he'll encounter over the course of his career: someone who knows the path ahead just a little better than he does, has seen some of the snares, choking vines, and pitfalls.

And this is the thing about status—status is intimate. But getting the upper hand doesn't mean winning. The best teaching experiences, I've discovered, come from getting down to their level. And that's what I try to do.

"What do you want?" I ask him.

Huh?

"What do you want? Really? What is success to you?"

He gestures noncommittally. "Getting published."

"Okay," I tell him. "I've got published. So you want that?"

He nods.

"But that's not really it, is it?"

He's frowning now.

"Who here has been published?

A couple of hands go up.

"Are you happy? Is that it? Are you done?"

Now they titter. Then shake their heads. Of course not. If they were done, they wouldn't be here.

"Right. So. You want to do it again."

"And make money!" one of them calls out.

"Sure," I say, "you want money. And respect?"

More nods.

"You want to say to someone, don't you—not someone like *anyone* but someone like *a very specific person* in your mind—that you did it. You made it."

"Yes," Marwan whispers and I wonder who that is for him. A father? Another teacher who ripped him apart?

"It doesn't happen."

Now they're all frowning.

"Not like that. Not the way you want it to. Maybe you have a moment when you feel you're up. A rush of joy when you get an award. Or the thrill of signing your first book deal. But it isn't enough. It's hardly ever enough. Whatever that *thing* is that's telling you to do this ... it never tells you you're good enough. And if it does — *if* you think you are good enough — it means you've probably stopped trying."

"So what are we doing here?" Marwan asks.

"Good question."

"What do *you* want?" asks Graci.

"Better question," I smile. "Look, I've published stuff. Some of it's good, some of it's not as good as it could have been. I want to get better. I want time enough to work, time enough to think. I want interesting projects. Friends. Something in the bank in case it all goes pear-shaped."

This isn't what they wanted. But it's the best thing I can teach them.

"People get into writing for all sorts of reasons. Writers love making writing look sexy. But mostly writing isn't sexy. Those things I said I wanted? I have them now. It took a load of work and luck and people helping me out along the way. But those are the things that make me happy and okay when the writing gets hard."

"So how do we get them?" Marwan asks. Now he's listening. At last.

"The best question," I tell him, and now he smiles. "By paying attention. Taking it all in. Sorting out for yourself what works for you. I can't tell you how to make a million bucks but I can give you some tips to survive *being* a writer. So listen up, okay?"

He does.

And he'll go home with a smile on his face.

And maybe next time he gets a rejection he'll hold it in his hand for a little longer, look at it, *really look to see what it's telling him*, before he stabs it with a nail.

But what about our CEO?

The CEO considers not going home. He could just keep driving, couldn't he? Let the road take him out of the city, drive to California where he wouldn't have to wear a suit. He could let his hair—what's left of it—grow out. He could wear leather sandals. He always thought the suit was protection, a kind of armor. But it isn't, he's learned. It's just a costume.

The doctor emerges from behind the sliding doors.

"Jamie's going to be all right," he says.

The CEO's face breaks into a smile. His muscles aren't used to it. He can almost hear them creaking. He takes the doctor's hand: warm, sweaty, and he pumps it up and down.

"Thank you," he says. "Thank you."

At home Deborah is folding the washing. She gently puts it away. This isn't what she wanted to do with her life. She had dreams of something else once. Dreams of being someone else. Dreams of being heard.

She places a folded shirt in the drawer.

Underneath it is a notebook.

She has been working at this for many months. In the early years of Jamie's life, time rushed past her—an undifferentiated mass. But now ... she jots down observations, little quips, things she has seen throughout the day. She doesn't know if it means anything. She doesn't know if it has to. Only that it is hers. Her world.

Downstairs she can hear her husband coming through the front door.

"Darling," he calls out. Is there something new in his voice? She thought he sounded strange over the phone. "I've got something to tell you ..."

She tucks the notepad away, knowing she will return to it. Whatever he says she will write it down. The pages will grow and grow and grow and then—who knows? Who knows what comes next?

Recommended reading. Keith Johnstone, *Impro: Improvisation and the Theatre* (originally published 1979).

DR. HELEN MARSHALL is a Senior Lecturer of Creative Writing at the University of Queensland. She has won the World Fantasy Award, the British Fantasy Award, and the Shirley Jackson Award for her two collections of short stories. Her debut novel, *The Migration*, released last year, argued for the need to remain hopeful, even in the worst circumstances. It was one of *The Guardian*'s top science fiction books of the year and was recently optioned by Clerkenwell Films.

Neowise

PAUL PARK

1. Last night the weather broke. A thunderstorm and then a new kind of air. A few of us climbed into the Forester and found a place above Chenail's farm, away from the lights of the town. We got out by the corn kiosk and stood in the deserted road, looking up toward Ursa Major in the Northwest, newly visible in the black, rinsed sky.

2. Often you can see a star more clearly when you look near it rather than at it. Doubtless this is a metaphor you have heard before, or used.

3. Doubtless also you are aware of the limitations of talking about writing, or any art form, as a series of prescriptions: do this, don't do that. This is how plot works. This is how you build a world. This is how you make an object come to life. While you are at it, no adverbs, unless … .

4. You speak with your mouth and part of your mind. The other part disagrees with everything you say, and is aware, for example, that you yourself pay no attention to the advice you give to other people. Writing is a different process for you, perhaps (though how could that be true?) — more intuitive. You clutch at images or moods. Everything mushed together. Nothing distinct. Perhaps a few fixed reference points, visible from time to time.

5. Tonight the air is clear. But what's that long, light smudge, down and away?

6. You want to see an image on the blank page of the sky. You want the night to teem with animals, people, objects, stories. You want them to persist even when the sun rises. Yet all you have is scattered, twinkling dots.

7. "I'm so pissed off," she said, smiling incredulously.

8. Writing is an indirect art form. The things we say scarcely matter in themselves. They are just reference points.

9. To make a character in a story come to life, to make them grow out of the words, to make them larger in the mind than they appear on the page, here's what you must do (or sometimes do, or never do—it doesn't really matter): Whenever we look at anything, we search for patterns and then things that don't fit. Assemble a human being out of the latter. Think for a moment about the various ways you are yourself, an object moving through space. You possess a physical form. You exist in four dimensions, with a future and a past. You are an object that behaves in certain ways, some repetitive, some erratic. You are an object in a complicated pattern of relationships with other objects, whose behavior affects your own.

10. She'd stepped away from the others and I could see only a bit of her, part of her cheek and her big nose, in the tiny light of her phone. Ignoring the comet, even though she'd been the one most eager to see it, she was talking instead to her ex-husband, a fool who had not earned a moment of her time.

11. "Oh, wow," said Jasper, pointing north toward the horizon.

12. You are an object that is also visible from inside itself. From that viewpoint you are able to manipulate, amid constraints that you might or might not be aware of, how you appear to others.

13. Outside the circle of light, moving over the surface of her face as she adjusted the position of her hand, I could only guess at the rest of her, a massed shadow. But I sketched it in: coarse black hair streaked with gray, big shoulders, a big eye. The slash of a black brow. Bruised lipstick, I knew—she never left the house without fixing it. Too much makeup always, demonstrating a level of precision that did not match her clothes, which always looked haphazard and thrown-on. Ripped jeans, tonight. Ratty T-shirt. But a Van Cleef bracelet, now invisible—onyx and gold. "That's just not true," she said into the phone.

14. A story about you, or else a story in which you appear, could be told either from the inside or from the outside. It doesn't matter which: in either case, imagine breaking apart those different aspects of an object, the different ways to describe it, and revealing them separately over time, as we do.

15. But it doesn't need to be said: the object can change during the course of the story, in any or all of these ways, depending on circumstances, choices, or a different understanding—or not. Or both.

16. Assemble a human being out of things that don't fit. Make these separate pieces of information contradict each other. Make them mutually exclusive. Make the object different from the way it is perceived. Give different observers conflicting impressions. Separate the image and self-image. Separate people from their own life story or their aspirations. Break apart what they are from how they behave. People are made of layers—separate them. People reveal themselves in bright and tiny specks of information, illuminated as if from within. Scatter them across the night sky. Make the rest of us work to see the repetitions, the patterns. Make us work to invent an image that will be unique to us, personal to us, because of what we bring to that process of invention. Ursa Major is a constellation of that sort.

17. "No," she said. From that one word I could extrapolate the entire conversation, which involved a struggle over shared custody, and a teenaged daughter's summer plans, interrupted now by the pandemic. And I knew she was lying when she turned to me, her face entirely obscured now with the light off. "Margot is such a pain," she said apologetically. "She's obsessed."

18. "Is she?"

19. An ambiguous gesture in the dark. "At least when it comes to the dry cleaning."

20. Jasper asked for the binoculars.

21. Let me rephrase what I just said: To make a character in a story come to life, here's what you must do (or sometimes do, or never do—it doesn't really matter): Whenever we look at anything, we search for patterns and repetitions, and then things that don't fit. Assemble a human being out of the former. The various ways we appear to ourselves and others, make them reinforce each other, make them aspects of the same thing. Do not let the pattern change, but instead strengthen it or clarify it over time as you add in more detail.

22. Such characters are like the Big Dipper, comforting because it is recognizable to all of us on the damp, cooling, asphalt road above Chenail's corn stand. Everybody sees the same one. (But what is that slashing blur, down and away?)

23. Many stories involve combinations of the two techniques. The difference is largely in our emotional response. The Big Dipper is part of Ursa Major. (I bet you saw that coming.)

24. People are made of disparate and contradictory elements, but we can always choose to portray them as if they are not.

25. An unnamed character in *Bleak House* exists for a single paragraph in a nine-hundred-page novel. Look how Dickens breaks apart the various pieces of information, with what economy he parcels them out, and observe the sequence of your emotional reactions (if any):

> "Judy, my child," says Grandfather Smallweed, "give this person his twopence. It's a great deal for what he has done."
>
> The person, who is one of those extraordinary specimens of human fungus that springs up spontaneously in the western streets of London, ready dressed in an old red jacket, with a "mission" for holding horse and calling coaches, receives his twopence with anything but transport, tosses the money into the air, catches it overhanded, and retires.

PAUL PARK is the author of a dozen novels in a variety of genres, and three collections of short stories. He is a senior lecturer in English at Williams College in Massachusetts and has taught the first week of the Clarion West workshop on multiple occasions: in 1998, 2000, 2002, 2006, 2008, 2011, and 2016.

The Old Marvellous

JOHN CROWLEY

I have been thinking about allegory recently, in no particularly rigorous way, since being invited to speak to the attendees at Mythcon 2020 in July; in the end I was unable to attend the con, and read my remarks over the Internet. (COVID had not yet brought Zoom into worldwide attention.) This piece is a modified version of what I read.

Some definitions are in order. Allegory in some ways resembles symbolism, and symbolism reflects metaphor, but isn't the same. Symbols can have actuality, can even have recorded histories, and can appear in varied ways in fictions. Lots of symbols live with us in our world: flags, monuments, uniforms, advertising icons. Cemetery sculptures have symbolic power: representations of resurrection, mourning, consolation. *Literary* symbols refer to matters within the story they furnish. In Michael Arlen's 1920s novel *The Green Hat*, the hat is a symbol for racy young people throwing off the previous generation's rules and prejudices. Metaphors can illuminate moments in stories, but refer to nothing but that illumination. *Allegories*, however, are fictional stories that exist only in that they are attached to other realities, other stories: moral commandments, the practice of justice and mercy, or truths that stand at a remove from and "higher" than the allegorical story that points to them. Often what is pointed to in an allegory is another more urgent or important story, usually one the reader knows in another context. A story out of the New Testament can be allegorized in a story set in the present day, or on another planet, while being itself an allegory of divine love or charity.

Allegory is likely the least loved of all literary forms, and even when the two tracks of the allegory are gripping in some way, the obviousness of the enterprise is always a little annoying. The writer attempting allegory needs to create an interesting and challenging story on the base level, while constantly allowing in pointers to the true matter, which in almost all allegories isn't fictional but moral, or political, or religious. C. S. Lewis wrote a great and lasting book, *The Allegory of Love*, about the possibilities of allegory through Western literature, and he wrote some allegories himself; in fact, it might be said that all his fiction was allegorical in some sense.

A key moment in the reading of an allegory (whether the reader perceives the story as an allegory or not) is the reader's growing awareness of what is allegorized. When I was in high school, sixty years ago, I read a couple of Lewis's planetary romances: *Out of the Silent Planet* and *Perelandra*. Lewis was even then admired and cherished by Catholics, lay and clerical, and though my family was Catholic, I read the novels because they were science fiction (it turned out they weren't). When I realized that they were actually *allegories*—though I didn't know much then about the category—I was deeply annoyed. What value was there in undercutting the aesthetics of SF, which in both books were striking and compelling, to produce what any Christian could easily decode? I knew the story of Adam and Eve; I understood the battle of the angels; I needed no lessons in the matter of original sin. Much later, I read *The Allegory of Love*, and then understood the attraction the SF project held for Lewis: the novels were what Lewis labelled "the marvellous-known-to-be-fiction." As he explains: "For poetry to spread its wings fully, there must be, besides the believed religion, a marvellous that knows itself as myth. For this to come about, the old marvellous must be stored up somewhere. Such a sleeping-place was provided for the gods by allegory, for gods, like other creatures, must die to live." The pagan gods, and the stories told of them, are mostly allegories of nature—astral objects, the oceans, vegetation, strife, death, sex—"whatever is begotten, born, and dies," as Yeats says. In the Western world, the allegorical gods come in time to be replaced (or at least sidelined) by growing monastic theology: by abstractions, named concepts like *Mens*, *Natura*, *Pietas*, *Amor*, etc. But those named concepts, when painted by Giotto, or called on to speak in medieval writings, take on the allegorical functions that the gods were forced to relinquish when they went to sleep. The visual representations of those theological abstractions, with their accompanying symbols, form in effect the allegory of an allegory.

The Christian belief is that nature is "fallen," and that our natures are not only implicated in the fall of nature, but brought about by our own fall into disobedience. The story events—snake, apple, fig leaf—can be understood as an allegory of that spiritual fall. Once, in a college ethics class taught by a Jewish refugee professor and biblical scholar, I disputed the value or force of that story; I did not believe we humans had been exiled from or deprived of a unified realm where all the other animals remained. But we *had*, he said; we came down out of the trees (!) and, over time, lost our original innocence, or ignorance; we came to know that we would die—all animals die, but other animals almost certainly don't envision it; we do, and that knowledge has been a vast force in human life on earth. We can't return to a place or time where we don't know we will die, or don't know we are naked. It might be said that the biblical story allegorizes the division of human consciousness from animal consciousness in the growing understanding that we are not in nature. An original perfection or "innocence" of which we were once a part was corrupted, both in the sense of putting nature to our own uses, and in our knowledge that we are born to die.

These two qualities of allegory—the story told and the matter it indicates—makes allegory both powerful and weak when deployed in fiction. What Lewis terms "the marvellous-known-to-be-fiction"—what the great Canadian critic Northrop Frye called "the secular scripture"—has gained immense power lately, partly due to advancing technologies of entertainment, but possibly also for more moral reasons. A lot of the fantasy films that deploy CGI and animation to create obvious versions of dozens of ancient stories can be called allegories—but allegories of what? Figures derived from Adam and Eve certainly turn up with some frequency in the new storytelling, as do battles of good angels and evil angels, God and Satan, dark and light, Heaven and Hell in a thousand forms, some using those old signifiers directly, some not; but insofar as they are versions of the Christian or biblical stories, the new stories can also be seen as allegories of an allegory. I've often thought that while realist fictions are full of struggles between persons whose moral and spiritual parts are mostly hidden or unfixed, liable to change as plots evolve, *fantasy* fiction gets to embody the same moral or spiritual energies in things—not only in weapons, a big category, but in magic helpers, recovered ancestral gifts, journeys of courage, all of it shown on the surface: in symbolic things the inside is made outside, and outside actions and powers allegorize the inside. Allegory in this sense is easy to use but hard to make new. Superheroes who sin and lose their powers and become ordinary mortals (for a time) are instantly interpretable: we get it.

Belief systems of many kinds present their tenets and their stories as actually existing or occurring in the world: in the beginning of everything; or in the time of the reception of the faith and its new description of reality; and also now. These assumed existent things—divine or supernatural beings and their activities and operations—can be allegorized secondarily in stories that restate, in more obvious or accessible forms, the mystic truths and beings that abide in a primary realm of their own. Over time, such a belief system can lose its grip on the imagination *as a set of actualities* and in effect become immured in the "sleeping-place of the gods" that Lewis defined. Linguistic or artistic allegories that were at first adopted solely as pointers or codes to aspects of divinity or morality can, in the end, comprise all there is of the system. What is interesting to me is that when a realm of divine beings, laws, activities, and judgments passes away, its *allegorical* power, which now points to nothing but itself, doesn't necessarily lose its *spiritual* power.

Take gnosticism, which comes in many flavors and offers more than one example of this process. Central to many gnostic systems is the belief that we humans are divine beings who once inhabited a realm of light outside the physical cosmos. We suffered a fall or an eviction from that realm (different gnostic sects give different reasons for this fall) and were cast into the dark and cold realm of the physical, and the physical body. Mandaean gnosticism posits numerous dark worlds into which the soul can sink, getting ever farther from "the house of my parents" and "lost among the worlds." I was very moved by the Mandaean system and its more sophisticated forms when I learned about it. I turned what I got from it and similar gnostic teachings not only into the underlying affective structure of a book, but the source for a comic strip that a character in the book follows: *Little Enosh, Lost Among the Worlds*. The Mandaean cast of characters became characters in the strip: Enosh (sometimes Anosh or Enoch in the original texts) is a spaceman, appearing to be a young boy who wanders in worlds where he is never at home. On these planets Enosh is caught and imprisoned over and over (as he is in gnostic imagining) by Rutha, an evil queen, sometimes Ruha in the texts, and her bad-guy gang, the Uthras, who aren't exactly bad guys in the original myth. Rutha wants, above all, for imprisoned Enosh to admit she is his mother, but he won't, because she isn't. Enosh is rescued from the Inn of the Worlds (an actual Mandaean term for the dark and confining universe we live in, or have been "thrown into" as the texts have it) by his actual mother, Amanda d'Haye, whom I derived from the Mandaean figure Manda d'Hayye, who is personified knowledge from the Worlds of Light. I pictured her as resembling Olive Oyl. Enosh in his spaceship is reminiscent of *Calvin and Hobbes*'s Spaceman Spiff. I've never had more fun in writing than I did in creating *Little Enosh* and learning how the Mandean texts could form the allegorical background of ordinary modern people and doings.

Not all allegory is religious, but it does seem to require a certain seriousness, at least for its original readers (or viewers: pictorial art can be allegorical, in some ways more easily than story can; see William Blake). Nor does allegory have to be extensive. An example would be the Owl of Minerva. Hegel, whose conception it is, says that the Owl of Minerva takes wing only at dusk. What he intends to express (almost all allegories need explication) is that only in its decline can we understand the true nature of a society or an age or an epoch. Minerva's owl comprises Minerva's attributes of wisdom, reason, memory. Its flight in the grey dusk is used not only to stand for the decline, and conceive the fall, of an age, but also to perceive the qualities of the epoch or age to come. Minerva's owl flies at a time when an old age is dying and a new age is struggling to be born. Minerva's owl could be called a metaphor, but it seems to express too large an idea to be simply that. It's an allegory: it wakes, it perceives the dusk, it flies, it knows the night and is certain of the dawn.

I recently read a long and fascinating piece in the *New York Times*: It tells of an unmarried, "spiritual but not religious" professional in her early thirties, who moved out of her communal house and into a convent of the Sisters of Mercy. A bunch of friends went with her. They called their project "Nuns and Nones," and they were the "Nones"—progressive millennials, none practicing Catholics, most interested in some form of social justice work. Millennials are the least religious group in America—only 27 percent attend religious services weekly. These young people, mostly women and a few men, were seeking ways to live radical activist lives, lives of devotion to their causes. The sisters began to see that the millennials wanted a road map for life and ritual, rather than a belief system. On one of the first nights, Sister Judy Carle said, one of the young people casually asked the sisters not what they believed but "What's your spiritual practice?" Ritual, story, commitments to practice, and spiritual friendship meant more than dogma, even when some of the Nones turned seriously to Catholicism, even if not—in some sense—to belief.

Two things struck me about this story. First and most obvious was its resemblance to, or reproduction of, early monasticism: the Benedictine joining of prayer and work (*laborare est orare*, to work is to pray) and the retreat of so many men and women from a collapsing world into safety and sense as much as into prayer and worship. There's evidence that millennials are less interested in, or occupied by, prospects of love, offspring, the family unit, the good job than any similar population before them. And I had also begun to wonder if the "believed religion" (Lewis's term) of most of the West in the last 2000 years is itself now becoming the "old marvellous-that-knows-itself-as-myth" (as Lewis says of paganism) and will itself have to undergo the same resurrection: it may have to die to live. The central stories, practices, arts of what might be called "ceremonial Christianity" (as opposed to the bare Christianity of, say, Unitarianism or Quakerism) might survive the religion itself, while the belief system and the cosmos it expresses will revert to Lewis's "sleeping-place provided by allegory." Terry Eagleton, former Marxist literary critic, now Christian thinker, has said that "a sacrament is a sign that accomplishes what it signifies." I am thinking that an allegory—even the allegory that points to something no longer stable or powerful—might be regarded as a story which produces the realm that governs what it tells.

JOHN CROWLEY was born in 1942 in an Army hospital in the appropriately liminal town of Presque Isle, Maine. He learned to read early. In high school and college he wrote poetry and fiction, and after graduation moved to New York City, where he worked in documentary film production and wrote three short SF novels: *Engine Summer*, *The Deep*, and *Beasts*. He moved to Massachusetts in 1979, and there completed a long fantasy novel, *Little, Big: or, The Fairies' Parliament*. Others followed, to the number thirteen. He taught others about writing fiction at Clarion, and also at Yale for twenty-five years, retiring in 2018.

The Three Laws of Great Endings and My Two Shameless Hacks

JAMES PATRICK KELLY

Three laws. The hardest part of writing a story is finding your way to its best ending. Lucky you if you know it right from the start. Most of us don't. We start with a character or a situation, an idea or a world. And whatever unknown force has prompted us to start this particular story at this particular time carries us along—until it doesn't. At some point, especially for headlight writers like me, the plot shifts or the protagonist finds her voice or a theme emerges, and the story begins to teach us what it means. But even a slight misstep at the ending can bring the whole enterprise to grief.

I'm no Isaac Asimov or Arthur C. Clarke, but I've always aspired to proclaim my own three laws. So here they are:

First Law
All great stories have great endings.

Second Law
A story which reads great until its flawed ending is just an okay story.

Third Law
A great ending will overshadow the flaws of a story which is otherwise just okay.

Now there is no surefire way to discover a great ending, but here are two writing hacks that may point toward the *best* ending for your story. They can work whether you already have a complete story with a wonky ending or are suffering a mid-draft meltdown because you have no clue how to find the exit.

Hack the first: ending dissection. For the purposes of this hack, dissect your ending into three parts: climax, resolution, and denouement. I have idiosyncratic definitions of these parts, so bear with me. There may be more than one climax in your story; what I'm referring to here is the very last one, the decisive moment in your plot, often but not always involving intense change and action. Then, because of this last climax, the narrative momentum slows as your characters find themselves in a new reality; they may or may not adjust to it. This is the resolution. The denouement is where characters point to a way forward after the story ends and, in the process, they (or perhaps only you) clarify the themes of the story and spin its meaning for the reader.

Let's take a quick look at some well-known examples. In *Hamlet*, the climax comes when Hamlet, after much dithering, takes his revenge on Claudius during the duel with Laertes. The resolution comes as the massacre plays out with Laertes and Hamlet dying as a result of Claudius's treachery. In the denouement, the survivors, Horatio and newcomer Fortinbras, sort things out and elegize Hamlet, who we learn has, in the end, "proved most royal." In *The Great Gatsby*, the process takes longer. The climax comes when George murders Gatsby in his pool. The resolution comes in the aftermath of the funeral as Nick realizes how friendless and alone Gatsby was. During this extended resolution, what Nick learns about Gatsby's past sets up a resonance with the idea of the American Dream, symbolized by the green light at the end of Daisy Buchanan's dock. The denouement tells us that chase it as we might, we will always be "borne back ceaselessly into the past" and away from that dream.

So, now it's your turn. As you plan for your ending, is there a final action that creates a new situation for your characters? Is it intense, or at least unmistakable? Will the reader be able to understand why everything must change because of it? If so, you have a climax. Now what is everyone going to do about it? Your characters' immediate reactions are key; knowing their future plans might also be helpful. What needs to be explained in light of the climax? But you're not done yet! What about a denouement? What did the story mean to the characters? Or to you? What, besides the plot summary, was it about? Some writers fear or eschew the "T" word, but if *theme* isn't your thing, ask yourself what spin you want to give the ending so that the reader will still be thinking about it next Thursday.

Hack the second: over-ending. In order for this hack to work, you must follow my instructions exactly. Don't worry, they are based on sound scientific principles that I've just made up. Your job is to make up ten different endings to your story (but there's a catch). If you already have an ending, that can be your ending number one. If you don't, however you thought you might end the story, even if you hated it, will be your number one. Going forward with the hack, as you develop new endings, you should refer to whatever you have already written. The new endings must reflect what has come before.

Now here's the catch: you must spend at least twenty-four hours on this process. For example, you might find endings two, three, and four come pretty quickly. That's okay. Maybe ending two is the opposite of ending one. Hamlet is never pricked by the poisoned sword and Gatsby survives his wounds. In order to generate the first three endings, you should only make changes either to the climax, resolution, or denouement. But depending on the density of your draft, ending attempts five, six, and seven might be harder to come up with. Take your time! After all, you have twenty-four hours.

As you go deeper into the process, it may occur to you that a change on page twenty-three or deleting the sex scene, might open up a new batch of endings. What if Ophelia didn't die? Maybe Rosencrantz and Guildenstern come clean to Hamlet? Deep revisions are permitted, but not before you come up with ending number five. As you get desperate to conjure endings, some of your new ideas may strike you as silly. That's good! Frustration is progress, and you are but mad north-north-west. When the wind is southerly, you'll know a hawk from a handsaw! So get a good night's sleep before you tackle endings eight, nine, and ten. Chances are very good, sez me, that one of these late endings will be the one you want.

Why does this work? Because of my spurious scientific principles which, often as not, work for me. What this hack does is to get your subconscious focused on the problem. Your rational, ordered, and conscious mind may well be locked into the parameters you decided on when you started writing. Of necessity, these tend to harden as you write. Your subconscious is not so constrained. I tend to think of my subconscious as the Little Guy who works on my fiction when I'm doing something else. Some also call her the Story Fairy. For me, he is likely to shake me out of a dream at four a.m. with the perfect plot twist, or explain how a misheard song lyric provides exactly the right character note for my antagonist. You definitely want him working with you and, in my experience, the more frustrated I am, the harder he works. This is why you need to take twenty-four hours, because if she's like my Little Guy, your Story Fairy works nights.

Resonance. You may perhaps feel uncomfortable resorting to such shameless writing hacks. Surely your sacred writing process must arise from a place that has nothing to do with checklists and mechanical stunts. Well, yes. I make no claim that they will get you a great ending. Remember that I said only that these hacks "may point toward the *best* ending for your story." Greatness in all its ineffable literary aspects remains a mystery to me; if I knew how to turn it on, believe me, I would! But I have a notion of what makes a great and magical ending. I say it is resonance.

Most stories are like your dreams. They may be vivid and exciting while you experience them, but at the end of the last sentence, they begin to shimmer and fade. Some people claim that they don't dream, or at least that they can't remember their dreams, and that may be so, but there are a handful of dreams, some recurring, a few one-shot, that I remember. They resonate. A great story with a great ending resonates. You remember it weeks, months, years after you read it. You recommend it to your friends. You reread it to understand why you're still thinking about it. You may even feel its influence when you reach an impasse in your current work in progress.

As I've thought hard about resonance over my career, I've developed my own personal list of examples and varieties of resonance. It is by no means exhaustive, and I don't claim to understand why these works resonate, only that they do for me. There is *resonance of voice*, which you can find in anything by Raymond Chandler, in Joseph Heller's *Catch-22*, and in Twain's *Huckleberry Finn*. In a story with *resonance of argument*, the reader will want to continue interrogating its polemical claims long after they stop reading. I think George Orwell's *Nineteen Eighty-Four* is an excellent example, as is Tom Godwin's controversial story "The Cold Equations" (by the way, if you're looking for an example of the third law of great endings, look no further than Godwin's clunky masterpiece). Readers are often exhausted by their surge of feeling in works which evoke a *resonance of emotion*, as in Shakespeare's *Othello* or novels by the Brontë sisters: Emily's *Wuthering Heights* or Charlotte's *Jane Eyre*. *Resonance of idea* is akin to resonance of argument, but in these works the central conceit is not necessarily meant to persuade so much as it is to engage the reader's imagination, as in Frank Herbert's *Dune*, Ursula K. Le Guin's *The Left Hand of Darkness*, and David Mitchell's *Cloud Atlas*. I'm not quite sure how to describe *resonance of transcendence*, but I can tell you that Arthur C. Clarke's *Childhood's End* and Charlie Jane Anders's *All the Birds in the Sky* — to name two very different novels — seem to me to be exemplars.

I will end this as I began. The hardest part of writing a story is finding your way to its best ending. But once you get there, dare to be great!

I wish you luck.

JAMES PATRICK KELLY has won the Hugo, Nebula, and Locus awards; his fiction has been translated into twenty-one languages. He writes a column on the internet for *Asimov's Science Fiction*. He was a member of the faculty at the Stonecoast Creative Writing MFA Program, 2005–2018, and has taught at both Clarions and the Odyssey Writing Workshop.

Diversity Plus: Diverse Story Forms, Not Just Diverse Faces

HENRY LIEN

As a gay Taiwanese immigrant (and vegan) writer, I get invited a lot to talk about diversity.

One of the things I've noticed is that discussions about representation and diversity in the arts today focus on diverse characters and creators. As crucial as that is, diversity can (and should) also include different story forms drawn from diverse traditions. Values are not universal across all cultures, and thus, the form that a satisfying story takes in one culture might be radically different from the forms in other cultures.

Lenses. Let's play a game. I'm going to use a very traditional Chinese/Taiwanese lens to describe two books that are well known here in the exotic Occident. Guess the book (titles written backwards).

1. Harmony is preserved in the empire through athletics.

   Let's dissect that a little. If we're looking at the story through a traditional Chinese/Taiwanese lens, we're assessing it from the viewpoint of a culture that values order and is wary of separatist provinces and ethnic minorities stirring unrest. Any activity that keeps the populace subjugated, especially one that directs potentially troublesome energy into something as wholesome as athletics, will be seen as a superb idea.

   Hint: *Semag Regnuh Eht*

2. One daughter marries the richest boy in her village, two marry paupers, the fourth ends up dead.

   Again, if we're looking at this through a traditional Chinese/Taiwanese lens, we're looking at a family that has no sons, has four daughters, is no longer rich, but is of high enough station that it would be a debasement for the daughters to seek the types of work available to women. In short, we're leering at a family as it careens toward generational decline. Traditional readers would be most concerned with whom the daughters marry and how they fare socially, not the daughters' own self-actualization as individuals.

Hint: *Nemow Elttil*

The point of this game is to show a) how vastly different cultural values can be, b) how those values in turn influence what is considered a satisfying story in that culture, and c) how true diversity in the arts can and should encompass diverse story forms in addition to diverse faces.

East Asian four-act story structure. The Western three-act story structure and the five-act Freytag pyramid variant are a) based on tension, conflict, and resolution and b) symmetrical in shape (ascent, climax, descent, plus a central question posed in the first act that is answered in the last act). This story structure is currently a popular feature of stories in the West, and we consider it a staple of a nourishing and satisfying storytelling meal. However, dietary tastes are learned and transmitted, and differ culture to culture. The same is true of story tastes.

The East Asian four-act story structure is radically different from the Western three- and five-act structures. It is common in Chinese, Taiwanese, Korean, and Japanese storytelling, although it is most known in the West by its Japanese name kishōtenketsu.

The structure is starkly different from Western structures.

ACT ONE —The Introduction of the Main Elements
ACT TWO —The Development of the Main Elements
ACT THREE —The Twist (New Element)
ACT FOUR —The Conclusion (Harmonizing of All Elements)

The Asian four-act structure is not necessarily based on conflict, tension, and resolution. It is more interested in exploring the unseen relationships among the story's elements than in pitting them against each other. It is also not symmetrical. The first two acts are characterized by a very gradual buildup. A radical twist appears in the third act that introduces a new element. The fourth act "harmonizes" all the elements that came before. By "harmonize," I don't necessarily mean a peaceful resolution. I mean that the fourth act contains a revelation about the relationships among the elements that often feels like a new element in itself.

The poet Sanyo Rai gave an elegant example of how this structure functions in a poem:

ACT ONE — Ki
The characters are daughters of Itoya in Osaka.
ACT TWO — Shō
The eldest daughter is sixteen and the younger one is fourteen.
ACT THREE — Ten
Historically in Japan, warriors have killed their enemy with bows and arrows.
ACT FOUR — Ketsu
However, the daughters of Itoya kill only with their eyes.

Now, that's a weird story. The first act introduces the elements of the two daughters and the setting. The second act just seems to develop those same elements. Thus, the entire first half seems to be a quiet, domestic story about life in feudal Japan. The third act injects a seemingly random element of war and violence, which comes as a surprise. The fourth act shows that the elements in the first two acts, the daughters, actually do have a relationship with the new third element, in that they are able to defeat them. The location of the surprise element so late in the story creates a more powerful sense of surprise. The fourth act harmonizes the preceding elements by showing the relationship among the elements in a way that itself feels like a new element (possibly a supernatural one). Adding a new element so late in the story is frowned upon in the Western three- or five-act structures. However, the late introduction of the new element creates a lingering effect. The story abruptly stops without answering all the questions, which causes the reader to continue thinking about it afterward. Do the daughters literally kill with their eyes? Are they sorceresses? Or was this metaphorical, like some sexist stereotype of girls seducing soldiers with their eyes only to murder them in their sleep? We don't know. We'll never know. As a result, we are left participating in the story by perpetuating it beyond the end of the page, and by writing potential explanations for its ending. The story lives on in a way that wouldn't be possible with a less abrupt ending.

My Neighbor Totoro. Let's look at *My Neighbor Totoro* as a case study. In case you haven't seen it, *My Neighbor Totoro* is a beloved animated film by Hayao Miyazaki about two young girls who move to the countryside to be near their mother who is recuperating in a hospital. The girls discover that the woods next to their new house is inhabited by benevolent supernatural owl-bear creature spirits. (It is an utter masterpiece. If you haven't seen it, it's available to stream on HBO Max in the US and on Netflix in all other territories.)

SPOILERS FOLLOW

To appreciate how different *My Neighbor Totoro* is from just about every Disney, Pixar, or DreamWorks animated film, let's list some of the things that it doesn't have:

- a villain
- a real central conflict
- a dead mother
- sibling rivalry
- adults who "just don't understand" or who have to be taught a life lesson by their children
- adults who disbelieve their children when they report that they've encountered the supernatural
- an empowerment character arc
- a third-act confrontation and action sequence

In short, *My Neighbor Totoro* has none of the basic story pieces with which just about every Western animated film is built. Instead, it has:

- siblings who don't bicker and who like each other
- parents who go with the flow when their kids tell them they've encountered the supernatural
- monsters that are neither frightening nor farcical
- what might qualify in Western storytelling as a shameless final-act deus ex machina
- characters who don't really have flaws
- characters that barely change, if at all

All of this sounds like instructions for how not to write a successful story. In fact, *My Neighbor Totoro* follows kishōtenketsu, which is not based on conflict, tension, and resolution.

ACT ONE (Ki) introduces us to Satsuki and Mei, their father, and their new house.
ACT TWO (Shō) has the sisters exploring their world and beginning their excursions with Totoro and Catbus.
ACT THREE (Ten), the twist, is when the girls learn something is wrong with their mother, and Mei becomes separated.
ACT FOUR (Ketsu) brings all the characters back together, weaving together the fantasy plot and characters with the domestic health scare (Totoro and Catbus take Satsuki and Mei to their mother), and shows us life for the family once the mother recovers and returns home.

Part of the power of *My Neighbor Totoro* is that it builds a world that is wholly benevolent around Satsuki and Mei. The old house, the woods, and the spirit creatures that populate them mean the girls no harm. The movie creates a warm glow around these girls and their world in the first two acts. When the very minor health scare (Mom has a cold and can't come home this weekend) comes in act three, it feels like a fiery asteroid has dropped into the girls' world. The shock of that small realization that there is darkness and loss in this world is heightened because there was no gradual ramp-up to it. Things that seem small to adults can be devastating to children, and the movie's use of kishōtenketsu makes it possible for adult viewers to feel like a child.

Act four sees all the elements in the story (Mom's health scare, the benevolent supernatural creatures) harmonizing. The supernatural creatures from acts one and two solve the unwelcome problem introduced in act three. The ultimate effect of this is that it lifts the curtain from childhood only a bit. It gives the girls only a little glimpse that unhappy things exist in this world. But then it drops the curtain again, telling them that they don't have to worry about that yet. Right now, the world is still a safe place, and they are allowed to be kids for just a while longer.

My Neighbor Totoro achieves these emotional effects through kishōtenketsu. If this were a traditional Western three-act structure, the health scare would have had to be foreshadowed more heavily, in the interests of symmetry. The foreshadowing would have resulted in a more gradual ramp-up to the very minor health scare, entirely robbing it of the devastating emotional impact it has. Making the health scare more serious wouldn't have solved the problem either. If the threat to their mother's health or life had been more serious, the film would never have been able to convincingly return to this precious feeling of safety by the end of the story.

Like all good structures, kishōtenketsu can work simultaneously on a macro and a micro scale. Not only does the overall story of *My Neighbor Totoro* follow kishōtenketsu, but many of the individual scenes within the story follow it on a scene level. Take, for example, the early part of their arrival at the house.

ACT ONE (Ki) — Satsuki and Mei explore their rickety old house.

ACT TWO (Shō) — They find that nature seems to have overtaken the house, with its rotted verandah, enormous camphor tree, and acorns falling from the ceiling boards.

ACT THREE (Ten) — They unlock the bath to momentarily glimpse hundreds of mysterious black creatures.
ACT FOUR (Ketsu) — Their father comes into the scene and explains that they're probably soot gremlins, which you sometimes see when you go from a bright place to a dark one.

In a Western animated film, this scene would probably be structured thus:

ACT ONE — Girls explore house to find ominous signs of soot gremlins.
ACT TWO — Girls have frightening, action-filled confrontation with soot gremlins.
ACT THREE — Girls' father dismisses their fears as imagined, setting up for a resolution in which the girls teach their father a life lesson about the importance of believing.

Eyerolls and yawns.

Kishōtenketsu is just one example of a diverse storytelling form, and *My Neighbor Totoro* just one example of a story embracing that form yet finding an audience in the West. I'd love to see a whole lot more. I'd invite storytellers to give themselves permission to learn about other story forms outside of their own cultural tradition. I'd urge readers and gatekeepers to open their minds about what a satisfying story can look like.

The world is a big place. Beauty comes in many forms. We talk a lot about how diversity is beautiful. Let's also start talking about how beauty is diverse.

HENRY LIEN is a 2012 graduate of Clarion West. He is the author of the Peasprout Chen middle grade fantasy series. His short fiction has appeared in publications including *Asimov's*, *Analog*, and F&SF, and he is a four-time Nebula/Norton Award finalist. Henry also teaches writing, including for the UCLA Extension Writers Program, and won the UCLA Extension Instructor of the Year award. Henry has previously worked as an attorney and fine art dealer. Born in Taiwan, Henry currently lives in Hollywood. Hobbies include writing and performing campy science fiction/fantasy anthems, and losing Nebula and Norton Awards.

Researching Imaginary Worlds

KEN MACLEOD

> "Research? We don't use that word in our house. We call it the 'R' word."
>
> — IAIN M. BANKS

If you're reading this you probably want to write science fiction and/or fantasy. Both are set in worlds different from our everyday consensus reality.

If you're writing about imaginary worlds, why do you need research? Why not just make it all up?

Let's take it, for our purposes here, that SF is speculative fiction set in a naturalistic universe, where minds run on top of material processes; fantasy is speculative fiction set in a non-naturalistic universe, where material processes run on top of an irreducibly mental reality. In fantasy, you can expect fate, prophecy, destiny, spells, and so on to work. In SF, not so much.

John Clute puts it differently, but compatibly: SF is an *argued* departure from consensus reality. It's set in the future, or in an alternative history, or another planet, or another universe. Fantasy is an *arbitrary* departure in the sense that it doesn't have to rationalize why it's telling a tale so far from the world we know.

When my daughter was very young, I used to read *Lord of the Rings* to her, and she asked: "When does it happen?" Christopher Tolkien was visiting a local bookshop to promote a new edition of his father's trilogy, so we asked him.

He replied: "I suppose the only answer I can give is: it happens in the Third Age of Middle Earth."

This was a much better answer than mine, which had been: "Uh, maybe the Pleistocene?"

Within SF broadly defined, there's a narrower field which critics have called "genre SF." It's what most people mean when they talk about SF. It's written by writers who know they're writing SF, and who themselves read SF and regard what they write as part of SF.

SF in general was invented in 1818 by Mary Shelley, with *Frankenstein*. (And if you read her introduction, you can see that she knew she'd invented something new in literature.) Genre SF was invented in the 1920s by the serial entrepreneur, inventor, and editor Hugo Gernsback. His formula for it was: "a thrilling romance which conveys scientific fact with prophetic vision," i.e., popular narrative form, scientific accuracy, and exploration of consequences. These are the rules of the game of genre SF, which you can break, but it's better (in terms of where to send your story, for one thing) to know you're breaking them. If you're writing genre SF, it really matters to salt your fiction with at least a grain of scientific fact, and to get that right.

Many otherwise educated people are surprisingly ignorant of quite elementary science. There's no shame in this. I was startled to read in an essay by Samuel R. Delany that in one of his classes he found students who didn't know that planets orbit the Sun, and that the Sun is a star and other stars might have planets. Some years later I was asked to judge a local literary society's science fiction story contest, and found even more incredible ignorance. But—as I sighed and decided to leave scientific accuracy entirely out of how I rated the stories—I reflected that I myself had got to a fourth year of studying zoology at university, and was *specializing in vertebrate paleontology*, when I discovered that I had only the vaguest notion of the history of life on Earth, and didn't know my Cretaceous from my Carboniferous. When I admitted this to my tutor, he kindly advised me to start by reading children's books on the subject. I did, and I can recommend it to you if you find yourself in that situation. After all, I got my degree!

Once you've got beyond simple introductions for the young—hopefully by having already read them when young, but as I say there's no shame in starting there if you haven't—it helps to have some general knowledge of science, and to keep up to date.

Google and Wikipedia are obvious places to start, but not to finish! The trick with Wikipedia is to follow the links to the sources (and to avoid falling into rabbit holes along the way). Google Scholar is useful in finding current (and historic) academic work in the sciences and the humanities, likewise

Google Books. You can read first-hand public communications from scientists in all fields at Scienceblogs.com. NASA and JPL have made available all the planetary and space science you'll ever need, from basic introductions to the latest pictures from Pluto and this week's trawl of exoplanets. But online research, however useful if you know what you're looking for (and there's the rub), can only take you so far. To judge the reliability and relevance of what you find, and to know what to look for in the first place, you still need to read books.

In any field of natural or social science or humanities, you can treat second-hand first-year college and university textbooks as the series bible of reality. If these aren't handy, you can look for any popular work that has been well reviewed by experts in that field (and, preferably, written by one). Then, if you want to know more, look at the back of the book — textbook or popular — for the bibliography and references, and then read whatever looks useful from the list. And if you want to go deeper, you look for *their* references. And so on.

When Iain M. Banks claimed not to do research, he was of course joking. The truth was he read so much about science, technology, and the world in general that when he sat down to write, he already had all the knowledge he needed. Even the imaginary science of his novels — the workings of faster-than-light travel, the power of energy weapons, and so on — had all been figured out beforehand and written down in careful notes and tables for handy reference.

Most SF writers keep up with current science to varying degrees. Some writers may lay themselves open to the suspicion of sneaking peeks at lab notes. For the rest of us it ranges from Stephen Baxter's reading of current research reports in scientific journals, through Peter F. Hamilton's weekly reading of *New Scientist* from cover to cover, to William Gibson's "I read my wife's fashion magazines (lots of good material there, really)."

If you're writing stories set in a plausible future, especially a near future, it's well worth reading the weekly *New Scientist* and/or the monthly popular science magazines *Discover* and *Scientific American*. The flagship science journal *Nature*, while more expensive, is more readable than you might expect. For current affairs, reading a daily broadsheet newspaper, supplemented perhaps by *The Economist* (available in many public libraries) is useful. All these, of course, are available online, with some content free to read.

When creating an imaginary world, you need to know about the real one, even if only to get a feel for its diversity and complexity. A flick through a random issue of *National Geographic* can introduce you to landscapes, customs, and organisms stranger than those found on many imagined alien worlds. Travel if you can possibly afford it. Take photographs. Make notes. I make no comment on the tax advice I got from one SF writer when I said I was saving up for my holidays: "Holidays? Writers don't have holidays! They have *research trips!*"

For research on specific topics, the trick is to read more than you need. That way, you'll have a wide choice among possible details to include in your story. And not just science! Read widely, in fiction and nonfiction. A quote you'll find attributed to me, though I'm sure it's not original, is "History is the trade secret of science fiction." History is an endless source of inspiration for plots, politics, and polities. As we all know, Isaac Asimov used Gibbon's *Decline and Fall of the Roman Empire* as source material for the Foundation series. The rise and fall of a galactic empire has by now become a trope. But history is full of far stranger and less familiar stories than that—take a browse through the *Penguin Atlas of World History* for strange maps and forms of rule other than cookie-cutter "kingdoms" and "empires."

Plunder your own experience. Every writer should have at all times a notebook slim enough for a shirt or back pocket or a purse. When an idea or an observation strikes you, write it down. And don't throw your notes away, even if you have no immediate prospect of doing anything with them. If you've been writing things down and keeping the notes all your life, so much the better. Those embarrassing notebooks and diaries from your teen years? Gold mine! You don't have to treat these as sources, just as inspirations. Try reversing situations, sexes, professions of any real people in your notes; mix them up and see what comes out.

"OK, SF has science to draw on, but what's the equivalent for fantasy?" That's the bewildered question I once asked Freda Warrington's husband Mike while Freda was signing books. He pointed me to myth and legend, which was a good start. I would now add history, religion, scripture, folklore, fairy tale; anthropology and history of magic (and alchemy, witchcraft, etc.) for the kinds of magical systems people believed actually worked. Obviously if you want to write fantasy you have to read fantasy, but that's not what you draw on. Go to the source! As I like to say: "Walk past the shelves of fantasy trilogy bricks. Head for the black Penguins. Steal from the best."

(The black Penguins, of course, are the Penguin Classics. Other editions are available.)

Then take this material and *recomplicate* it. You can see this happening with the stories of King Arthur. Tennyson recast Malory who recast earlier works that recast Geoffrey of Monmouth who in turn ... And modern writers can derive tales from any of them, or they can imaginatively go back behind these sources and bring forward new stories as different as T. H. White's *The Once and Future King* and Rosemary Sutcliffe's *Sword at Sunset* and Jo Walton's *The King's Peace* and, for that matter, John Boorman's *Excalibur*.

The Russian writer Kirill Eskov is a paleontologist and the author of *The Last Ringbearer*, which you can only read online for reasons that may become clear. He once gave me a very paleontological explanation of recomplication:

"*The Lord of the Rings*," he said, "is heroic epos. What kind of society produces heroic epos? And in what kind of society is that heroic epos rewritten like the story we are told in *The Lord of the Rings*? The same kind of society as the one where Sir Walter Scott wrote *Ivanhoe*. His knights are protectors of the weak. Real knights were thugs and brutes! So we have to work back from the later society to the earlier society, and reconstruct how *that* society might have distorted what happened in its past, to get at the 'real story' of the events that inspired the heroic epos."

And then—in his case—you can turn that into a fantasy novel that purports to tell "the real story" of what happened after the fall of good king Sauron (champion of science and industry) and his bright realm of Mordor ...

Not that I'm suggesting you do that! The Tolkien estate is not to be messed with. What I am suggesting is that history and literature and the sciences are full of exciting ideas that can inspire new and original stories, and that the most important research is what you do before and between and after writing stories, and that is reading. Another quote you find attributed to me which probably isn't original is "The way to become a writer is to write, write, and keep on writing." This is true, in that you do have to actually write, write, and keep on writing.

What is not true is what I thought when I first said it, that you get better with practice. You get better with experience, which is not quite the same thing. You don't need to write a million words before you can write well. As Delany points out in *About Writing*, writing isn't a skill like that of a musician, a woodcarver, or an athlete, where practice really does make perfect. And writing certainly doesn't get any *easier* with practice; I can tell you that for nothing. I'm well into writing my eighteenth novel, and it's no easier than writing my first, second, third ...

You improve as a writer by learning consciously what to do and what not to do, learning to do things right and to correct mistakes. And the best way to do that is to learn from other writers. You can do this at workshops like Clarion and Clarion West, and you can do it all the time by reading.

The way to *remain* a writer is to read, read, and keep on reading.

KEN MACLEOD was born on the Isle of Lewis and now lives in Gourock, Scotland. He is the author of seventeen novels, from *The Star Fraction* (1995) to *The Corporation Wars* (2018), and many articles and short stories. He has won three BSFA awards and three Prometheus Awards, and been short-listed for the Clarke and Hugo Awards. He was a guest instructor at the Clarion West Summer Workshop in 2018. His most recent book is the novella *Selkie Summer* (NewCon Press, 2020). He is currently writing a space opera trilogy.

Something to Cry About

NISI SHAWL

During any given year I'll teach several classes on how to describe characters of color. Based on what I've seen in these classes and in my own reading, non-Afrodiasporic authors pay way too much attention to skin color in their descriptions of the Black community, and not nearly enough to our hair.

There are exceptions. Some do get it. A while back, a white man and I had a great talk comparing how different audiences reacted to his anecdote of a young Black woman falling into a swimming pool on the day she got her hair done. The white group he told it to said, "What a shame," "Bad luck!" Things like that. But the Black group shuddered visibly before expressing their horror.

Hair is important. In "Cruel Sistah," my Ebonicsization of a sixteenth-century Scots ballad, it's a motive for murder. Two sisters are rivals for the same man; he remarks how pretty the one he prefers is, with "the little drops of rain in her hair shining, and it stayed nice as a white girl's." But the jealous murderer's hair is "as naturally nappy as his, worse between her legs."

Hair texture really does vary this significantly between family members; I based "Cruel Sistah" on the friction between me and my sister Julie, whose "good" hair more than made up for her darker complexion in the eyes of her many admirers. Please be sure to take this sort of thing into account when telling readers what your characters look like and how others relate to their looks.

Genetic diversity can also make itself felt in different textures of the hair growing out of a single individual's scalp. Most Afrodiasporans are of at least minimally mixed blood. This also shows up in our wide range of skin tones, but don't forget the hair! Never forget the hair! By the time I was old enough to comb and braid my own hair, I'd been subjected to close analysis of my scalp and follicles by almost all my living female relatives. "She got good bangs," they agreed. "She all right in the front. But things back here is a little rough. That's why she so tenderheaded."

"Tenderheaded" is a term peculiar to twentieth-century African American culture. Little girls (and later, boys) getting their hair greased (yes, greased—we'll get to that in a minute) and combed and braided, a process often taking hours, were required to "Sit still!" between the knees of older women in whatever attitude those women found most convenient. Attempts to look at the television or massage an aching neck would be met with a sharp WHACK! of the instrument of torture against the child's head. Tears were met with threats to give her "something to cry about" (thus this essay's title).

That is how Black women of a certain age were trained from childhood to downplay and suppress our pain—and also, to a certain extent, Black men raised after the advent of the cornrows Stevie Wonder popularized. And it's part of the background of any believable fictional character of those demographics.

As I talk with people of other races I encounter similar unofficial training programs. But there are one or two hair-related points that are peculiar solely to Black culture, additional points of which writers must be aware. First, shampooing. Washing your hair, for a Black person, isn't something that typically happens every day, or every other day, or even every week. It's a Big Deal. Once a month, maybe. Black women plan for it, build itineraries around it, schedule their household chores and public appearances with shampoo times in mind. Write about it accordingly.

Second, grease. Grease is good! I was in the eighth or ninth grade before I realized that white people did things to deliberately get grease *out* of their hair, whereas in my neighborhood we were dolloping it on by the fingerful. Our suppliers included Posner's, Madam C. J. Walker, and Crown Hair Care, but plenty of people used plain old Vaseline.

And yes, nine times out of eleven the end result of being washed and greased and combed was being braided. As a special treat, though, those of us AFAB (Assigned Female At Birth) could take a trip to the beauty parlor for something nicer. The soothing ministrations of a professional hairstylist were a balm to be celebrated; the sizzling heat of a pressing iron or the tang of a chemical straightener were the lightest of trials, easily endured because they led to pipe curls, pageboys, and a dozen more white-imitating styles.

In my youth, these beauty parlor professionals occupied the apex of Black society, right up there with church deaconesses and school teachers. Any verisimilitudinous fictional account of Black characters' lives will reflect at least one of the myriad ways in which Black women, hair, and business have intersected, from Madam C. J. Walker's millionaire status through twenty-first-century immigrants' home hair-braiding services.

Wigs are another example of the interaction between Black culture and hair. Wig shops abound. Nothing shameful about wearing a wig, which may be a side effect of accepting the widespread prohibition against the hair you're born with: rule out what's natural, and artificial is the only way forward. My mother wore a wig with a blond streak in it all through the 1970s and 80s. My own hair is thinning with age; my friend Victoria comforted me by saying, "Guess you'll have to be one of those fancy ladies in wigs." Depicting this sort of frank, playful attitude can add depth to your depictions of Black characters.

It's possible to depict us. It's possible for even those who do it well to do it better.

White author Richard K. Morgan's Carl Marsalis, hero of his 2008 novel *Black Man*, is a near-perfect portrayal across racial lines. Marsalis's encounters with racial slurs, his attitudes towards authority, and his reflections on the sexual politics of beer commercials are all on target. But Morgan misses the bullseye when Marsalis removes a hat he has been wearing and it leaves no imprint on his afro.

Hat head is real. Genre conventions may transform the offending headgear into a space helmet or a crown or a be-goggled leather helmet, but its effect on certain sorts of hair—my sort—needs to be noted in your text.

Speaking of headgear, there's yet another way in which it's involved with Black hair—specifically, Black women's hair. In New Orleans during the late 1700s, it was illegal for a woman with even a smidgen of Black blood to be seen in public bareheaded. The so-called "Tignon Laws" mandated scarf-wearing, and though they've long been repealed, their influence lasts to this day. When K. Tempest Bradford Zooms with me, she's almost always tignoned. So am I, unless I've very recently done my hair—as in within the last four or five hours. Before I go out, before I allow my camera to send video of me, I simply must cover my hair. An injunction this old and this deeply engrained may remain potent into the next century, and well beyond it.

Am I giving all our secrets away? Maybe. Here, have some more.

Though I've titled this essay in honor of the pain I associate with the Black hair experience, it's not all grief. How many nerve endings are there in the human scalp? Thousands. A source of suffering can also be a source of pleasure. When I was little, girls I was getting to know would offer at a certain point to "play with my hair." This was an intimate privilege, extended only to special friends, those you truly clicked with. Hours and hours of gentle caressing passed between us, disguised as routine attention to basic hygiene. Including reflections on and depictions of such interactions will help your stories featuring Black characters ring real. That's what I want. That's what you want, too, right?

So here are some words to describe natural hair textures: good, fine, nappy, wooly, wavy, kinky, crinkly, crisp (a mostly nineteenth-century usage), and the term Nalo Hopkinson—another Black speculative fiction author—and I came up with: krinky.

(Not curly, please, unless we're discussing natural hair that is indistinguishable from that of a white person. I view use of this adjective as an attempt to erase some of the differences Black hair usually exhibits in terms of cross-section, surface, etc.)

Here are some words and phrases for styled and treated hair: pressed, hot combed, processed, relaxed, conked (a mostly 1950s and 60s usage), given a permanent, Jheri curled, plaited (pronounced *platted*), braided, French braided, cornrowed, dreaded, twisted, loc'd.

And here are a few more in-group haircentric words: bonnet, kitchen, pick, drycomb, edge-up, weave, extensions, fade, 'fro, puffs, waves.

I promise you that though some of the terms above may not seem that way, all of them are relevant to the work of describing hair coming out of African-descended people's heads. If necessary, use the internet to help you understand their meanings.

Finally, if you're writing about Black characters and mentioning their hair, you may want to touch on the topic of touching. Especially if your characters are women. This isn't exclusively Black territory, and not linked exclusively to gender, either, but ... I have not met one female-identified person of African descent who hasn't had to deal with random requests to feel her hair. Such requests come not just from new acquaintances but also from total strangers; not just from curious and under-socialized children but also from full-grown adults. And fairly often there's not even the civility of a request—only a pair of grabby hands appearing out of nowhere to reach for your head.

It's your call whether or not such an incident fits with the tale you're trying to tell. It's your call how you portray any of these points. But think them over. Please.

NISI SHAWL, winner of one Kate Wilhelm Solstice Award and two Locus Awards, wrote the 2016 Nebula Award finalist *Everfair* (Tor) and the 2008 Tiptree Award-winning collection *Filter House* (Aqueduct). They have edited and co-edited numerous anthologies such as the 2020 World Fantasy Award–winning *New Suns: Original Speculative Fiction by People of Color*. In 2005 they co-wrote *Writing the Other: A Practical Approach*, basis of an ongoing class series. Shawl helped found the Carl Brandon Society and serves on the board of the Clarion West Writers Workshop, of which they are a 1992 alumna. They live in Seattle and take frequent walks with their cat.

The Narrative Gift as a Moral Conundrum

URSULA K. LE GUIN

The narrative gift, is that what to call it? The storyteller's knack, as developed in writing.

Storytelling is clearly a gift, a talent, a specific ability. Some people just don't have it—they rush or drone, jumble the order of events, skip essentials, dwell on inessentials, and then muff the climax. Don't we all have a relative who we pray won't launch into a joke or a bit of family history because the history will bore us and the joke will bomb? But we may also have a relative who can take the stupidest, nothingest little event and make it into what copywriters call a gut-wrenchingly brilliant thriller and a laugh riot. Or, as Cousin Verne says, that Cousin Myra, she sure knows how to tell a story.

When Cousin Myra goes literary, you have a force to contend with.

But how important is that knack to writing fiction? How much of it, or what kind of it, is essential to excellence? And what is the connection of the narrative gift with literary quality?

I'm talking about story, not about plot. E. M. Forster had a low opinion of story. He said story is "The queen died and then the king died," while plot is "The queen died and then the king died of grief." To him, story is just "this happened and then this happened and then this happened," a succession without connection; plot introduces connection or causality, therefore shape and form. Plot makes sense of story. I honor E. M. Forster, but I don't believe this. Children often tell "this happened and then this happened," and so do people naively recounting their dream or a movie, but in literature, story in Forster's sense doesn't exist. Not even the silliest "action" potboiler is a mere succession of unconnected events.

I have a high opinion of story. I see it as the essential trajectory of narrative: a coherent, onward movement, taking the reader from Here to There. Plot, to me, is variation or complication of the movement of story.

Story goes. Plot elaborates the going.

Plot hesitates, pauses, doubles back (Proust), forecasts, leaps, doubling or tripling simultaneous trajectories (Dickens), diagrams a geometry onto the story line (Hardy), makes the story Ariadne's string leading through a labyrinth (mysteries), turns the story into a cobweb, a waltz, a vast symphonic structure in time (the novel in general) ...

There are supposed to be only so many plots (three, five, ten) in all fiction. I don't believe that either. Plot is manifold, inexhaustibly ingenious, endless in connections and causalities and complications. But through all the twists and turns and red herrings and illusions of plot, the trajectory of story is there, going forward. If it isn't going forward, the fiction founders.

I suppose plot without story is possible — perhaps one of those incredibly complex cerebral spy thrillers where you need a GPS to get through the book at all. And story without plot occurs occasionally in literary fiction (Woolf's "The Mark on the Wall," perhaps) — oftener in literary nonfiction. A biography, for instance, can't really have a plot, unless the subject obligingly provided one by living it. But the great biographers make you feel that the story of the life they've told has an aesthetic completeness equal to that of plotted fiction. Lesser biographers and memoirists often invent a plot to foist onto their factual story — they don't trust it to work by itself, so they make it untrustworthy.

I believe a good story, plotted or plotless, rightly told, is satisfying as such and in itself. But here, with "rightly told," is my conundrum or mystery. Inept writing lames or cripples good narrative only if it's truly inept. An irresistibly readable story can be told in the most conventional, banal prose, if the writer has the gift.

I read a book last winter that does an absolutely smashing job of storytelling, a compulsive page-turner from page 1 on. The writing is competent at best, rising above banality only in some dialogue (the author's ear for the local working-class dialect is pitch-perfect). Several characters are vividly or sympathetically portrayed, but they're all stereotypes. The plot has big holes in it, though only one of them really damages credibility. The story line: an ambitious white girl in her early twenties persuades a group of Black maids in Jackson, Mississippi, in 1964, to tell her their experiences with their white employers past and present, so that she can make a book of their stories and share them with the world by selling it to Harper and Row, and go to New York and be rich and famous. They do, and she does. And except for a couple of uppity mean white women getting some egg on their face, nobody suffers for it.

All Archimedes wanted was a solid place to put the lever he was going to move the world with. Same with a story trajectory. You can't throw a shot put far if you're standing on a shaky two-inch-wide plank over a deep, dark river. You need a solid footing.

Or do you?

All this author had to stand on is a hokey, sentimental notion, and from it she threw this perfect pitch!

Seldom if ever have I seen the power of pure story over mind, emotion, and artistic integrity so clearly shown.

And I had to think about it, because a few months earlier, I'd read a book that brilliantly demonstrates a narrative gift in the service of clear thought, honest feeling, and passionate integrity. It tells an extremely complicated story extending over many decades and involving many people, from geneticists cloning cells in cloistered laboratories to families in the shack-houses of Black farming communities. The story explains scientific concepts and arguments with great clarity while never for a moment losing its onward impetus. It handles the human beings it involves with human compassion and a steady, luminous ethical focus. The prose is of unobtrusive excellence. And if you can stop reading it, you're a better man than I am, Gunga Din. I couldn't stop even when I got to the notes—even when I got to the index. More! Go on! Oh please tell me more!

I see a huge difference in literary quality between these two hugely readable books, which certainly has to do with specific qualities of character—among them patience, honesty, risk-taking.

Kathryn Stockett, the white woman who wrote *The Help*, tells of a white girl persuading Black women to tell her intimate details of the injustices and hardships of their lives as servants—a highly implausible undertaking in Mississippi in '64. When the white employers begin to suspect this tattling, only an equally implausible plot trick lets the Black maids keep their jobs. Their sole motivation is knowing their stories will be printed; the mortal risk they would have run in bearing such witness, at that place in that year, is not seriously imagined, but merely exploited to create suspense. White Girl's motivation is a kind of high-minded ambition. Her risks all become rewards—she loses malevolent friends and a bigoted boyfriend and leaves Mississippi behind for a brilliant big-city career. The author's sympathy for the Black women and knowledge of their everyday existence is evident, but, for me, it was made questionable by her assumption of a right to speak for people without earning that right, and killed dead by the wish-fulfilling improbability of her story.

Rebecca Skloot, the white woman who wrote *The Immortal Life of Henrietta Lacks*, spent years researching a vastly complex web of scientific research, thefts, discoveries, mistakes, deceits, cover-ups, exploitations, and reparations, while at the same time trying, with incredible patience and good will, to gain the trust of the people most directly affected by the one human life with which all that research and profit-making began—the family of Henrietta Lacks. These were people who had good reason to feel that they would be endangered or betrayed if they trusted any white person. It took her literally years to win their confidence. Evidently she showed them that she deserved it by her patient willingness to listen and learn, her rigorous honesty, and her compassionate awareness of who and what was and is truly at risk.

"Of course her story is superior," says Mr. Gradgrind. "It's nonfiction—it's true. Fiction is mere hokum."

But oh, Mr. Gradgrind, so much nonfiction is awful hokum! How bad and mean my mommy was to me before I found happiness in buying a wonderful old castle in Nodonde and fixing it up as an exclusive gourmet B&B while bringing modern educational opportunities to the village children ...

And contrarily, we can learn so much truth by reading novels, such as the novel in which you appear, Mr. Gradgrind.

No, that's not where the problem lies. The problem — my problem — is with the gift of story.

If one of the two books I've been talking about is slightly soiled fluff while the other is solid gold, how come I couldn't stop reading either of them?

NOTE: With the consent of the author's estate, "black" is changed to "Black" for this reprinting.

URSULA KROEBER LE GUIN (1929–2018) was a celebrated and beloved author of twenty-one novels, eleven volumes of short stories, four collections of essays, twelve children's books, six volumes of poetry, and four of translation. The breadth and imagination of her work earned her six Nebulas, nine Hugos, and SFWA's Grand Master, along with the PEN/Malamud and many other awards. In 2014 she was awarded the National Book Foundation Medal for Distinguished Contribution to American Letters, and in 2016 joined the short list of authors to be published in their lifetimes by the Library of America.

Tapping the Source

ELIZABETH HAND

During a quarter century (!) of teaching creative writing, perhaps the single most important change I've seen in any individual's work is how much stronger it gets when they tap into their own personal experiences. This isn't necessarily *Write what you know* so much as *Write what you've felt*. While I've always drawn on my own life in my work, the first time I realized that readers related to a particular experience was with a short scene, about a page long, in my 1995 novel *Waking the Moon*. The eighteen-year-old protagonist, Sweeney, has been dropped off at college; it's the first time she's really been on her own in her entire life, other than childhood sleepovers with friends. Desolate in her isolation, she sits on the windowsill of her dorm room and wonders if she's made a terrible mistake in leaving home. For years, readers would tell me how deeply they related to that one scene, whether or not they'd gone off to college.

Without realizing it, I'd tapped into a widespread feeling among adolescents: that sense of loss and grief over leaving home and family, coupled with exhilaration at finally (*finally*) being on their own in a new place. I just reread the scene for the first time in decades and was struck by how many details it contained from my own first night alone. I'm not sure I could channel that 1975 experience as powerfully now, forty-five years later, as I did when I wrote the book, but rereading that page made me feel eighteen again: listening to even more homesick exchange students weeping down the hall, envying the older students who already had friends and places to go other than their unfurnished rooms. I'd always thought the primary job of the writer was to make things up, but with this revelation I realized that memory, both emotional and sense memory, were just as (if not more) important.

I can't recall when I came up with this two-part exercise/prompt, but it was at Clarion West or Clarion, and is specifically geared toward writers doing non-mimetic fiction. I've seen myriad authors come up with amazing stories using this technique. I still use it in workshops, usually over the course of several days.

Be aware that this exercise can involve recalling a difficult memory or experience. It can also involve a positive one: it's your choice. Great writing involves invoking powerful emotions and putting them into words: it's both a challenge and a responsibility, and also a great joy.

Using a negative experience can often provide more fodder for material. I think that's because any extreme negative experience evokes the fight-or-flight response, which puts us on sensory alert. In these circumstances, we can become hyperaware of our surroundings, and our senses can register smells, tastes, sounds, textures, sights more vividly than they usually do. The same thing can occur with positive experiences, though with these, we're often so much in the moment that, in memory, the event becomes a happy blur.

Or not. Everyone's sensorium is different. When I assign this two-part exercise, I have participants share their work by reading aloud, both Part One and Part Two. It can get very emotional, but in a good way. For a group of writers, it's a trust exercise. By sharing our best/worst experiences, we can glimpse the wellspring from which all great writing—which means honest writing—comes. I've done this exercise with writers of various ages, from teenagers to older adults. I always begin by stating that this is not an exercise in catharsis, nor is it meant to be therapeutic. Delving into difficult memories—or happy ones, if recalled during a difficult time such as our present pandemic—can be a highly emotional experience that can trigger sensitive people.

Yet the act of writing, at its best, involves evoking emotional responses in a reader—joy, sorrow, grief, delight, desire, terror, unease, hilarity, transcendence. Any act of creation also involves the risk of exposure, of rejection, of failure: not commercial failure but the near-constant (in my experience) realization that one's best effort still may not capture in words the vision in the writer's head. I believe strongly that a writer needs to trust herself, and learn, by writing, what level of risk she is comfortable with. Obviously, not all writing deals with profound emotions or trauma, and a light touch goes a long way when distilling one's experiences onto the page.

During the pandemic, which has isolated so many of us, it might be useful to do this exercise in tandem with a writing partner or small group. Sharing our deepest joys and fears isn't just a crucial part of being an artist: it's one of the most important parts of being human. Fiction can act as a filter and a buffer in difficult times. It can be a lifeline for those who are alone, or feel alone. If possible, find or create a writing community in which to share your work.

Part One: Recall your worst/best day at work. Write about it briefly—between one and three pages, no longer. Try to get down anything specific you recall of the event, in particular any sensory impressions. Don't try to write lyrically. You don't even need to bother writing in complete sentences, but do tell the story of your worst/best day on the job. Describe the event, the people involved (if any), and how you reacted at the time. Notice if you have vivid memories of the experience, and think about what aspects of it came back to you most clearly and most intensely.

Part Two: Take your nonfiction account, and turn it into a piece of flash fiction—one to five pages, no more—which in some way jumps off from the actual event. It does not need to adhere to the strict progression or narrative of your original nonfiction account.

Your story can be fantasy, science fiction, horror, magical realism, supernatural, slipstream, whatever you want to call it. The only thing it can't be is nonfiction or mimetic (non-fantastic) fiction. There has to be some element of fantastika. This is solely for the purpose of the exercise, to demonstrate how one can take raw experience and transform it into something that is seemingly light-years away from its source material. If later you want to write a straightforward or memoiristic account, go for it.

This story can involve all or only some of the original characters from your initial account. The setting can be the same or different, past or alternate present or future.

When I do this prompt in workshop, I always assign a theme, so that we can see how differently everyone interprets it. The theme I generally use is First Contact. You can interpret this however you choose: first contact with an alien, with a person, with a non-human species, with a place, a new job, a new relationship, a historic event, a scientific discovery, whatever. The notion of First Contact is extremely mutable and can allow for untold interpretations. Feel free to embellish as lavishly as you please when you write Part Two!

Since this is based on your own particular experience, you are pretty much guaranteed that you will produce a piece of fiction unlike anyone else's. The more specific you can be in recalling your initial details and making use of them, the more distinctive and personal the final work tends to be.

Good luck, and good writing!

ELIZABETH HAND is the author of sixteen novels and five collections of short fiction and essays, including *Waking the Moon*, *Glimmering*, *Wylding Hall*, and the Cass Neary series, featuring "one of literature's great noir antiheroes" [Katherine Dunn]. She is a longtime critic and reviewer for the *Washington Post*, *LA Times*, and *F&SF* magazine, among many others. Her most recent novel, *The Book of Lamps and Banners*, was released in 2020, and she's at work on a new thriller, *Under the Big Black Sun*, set in Hawai'i. When not sheltering in place, she divides her time between the Maine coast and North London.

Feed Your Engine

JACK SKILLINGSTEAD

If you're a writer, the train is always there, waiting at the station. Sooner or later you climb aboard.

You can't help yourself.

It's one of those old-time steam engines. A two-hundred-ton iron monstrosity. You know, like in the movies, where some poor shmuck has to keep shoveling coal into the furnace to keep the thing moving.

Before you actually pull yourself up the ladder and test the controls, you're like a silent-movie kid lying in the shade chewing on a piece of straw, skylarking the days away. The duration of your skylarking period will vary. But most writers pick up the shovel at a fairly young age. I started my serious shoveling at twenty-four. Plenty of people start younger. Some start much later. Raymond Chandler didn't do any of the serious work we know him for until he was into his forties. Annie Proulx, of *The Shipping News* and *Brokeback Mountain* fame, published her first novel in 1992. She was fifty-seven.

I can hear the wails of despair. Fifty-seven!

Don't panic. Her first short story appeared in 1963. She probably wrote it when she was twenty-seven or twenty-eight. Of course, she could have been shoveling coal since she was twelve, like Ray Bradbury. Usually you start working years before a first sale. By the way, Proulx's first published story appeared in a science fiction magazine called IF, edited by Frederik Pohl.

Anyway, back to the train.

Before you climb aboard, it's kind of fun to fantasize about being the engineer. Riding the rails to fabulous destinations. Mostly it's the destinations you're thinking about, rather than the shovel. Your byline in magazines, on the covers of books, maybe etched into the base of an award. Inhabiting the identity of: Professional Writer. Meanwhile, if you think about the shovel at all, it's in some romanticized fashion that probably has more to do with whatever your version is of a café on the left bank of the Seine. The shovel itself might take the form of a nice Montblanc pen, or if you want to get modern about it, a MacBook Air. I'm being a little facetious—but only a little.

Don't be fooled. Whatever your tool, it's still a shovel. And if you want to fulfil your destiny as a writer you will learn to pick it up and get to work—the sooner the better.

Okay. Why am I going on about train engines? Even *I'm* getting sick of this metaphor. But I want to impress on new writers that "being a writer" has a lot to do with a working-class mindset. You may love the act of writing or you may hate it, relishing only the having-written part. It's all the same. The train only keeps rolling as long as you keep shoveling. This is true in the beginning when you're struggling to discover your voice, and it's true later when you're established. If you stop working, stop producing, the train grinds to a halt.

This is why it's so remarkable when a writer of fiction enjoys a long uninterrupted career. Even if you love the act of writing, and many of us do, it can still be a real grind. Plucking those words out of thin air day after day. Revising, revising, revising. There's a tedious aspect to it. For instance, producing the first draft of a novel is only the first step to finishing a novel. When I look at NaNoWriMo (National Novel Writing Month) I think: fantastic! Grinding out a sufficient number of words every day to add up in one month to a novel-length manuscript is a real accomplishment.

But I also think: then comes the hard part.

The truth is, the less narratively coherent your first draft is, the harder it is to write the second draft. Your mileage will vary, but I can tell you that I wrote eight novel-length works before placing the ninth with a publisher. The first five of those of those books were written very much in the NaNoWriMo mode, before NaNoWriMo existed, though I was never that fast. I would determine a daily page count—three pages for some books, five pages for others. Whatever I thought I could handle. And then I'd set off with very little idea of what shape the story would take. By the end of the draft I would usually have lost control of narrative coherence. To say the least. Eventually I learned to do some thinking and planning ahead of time. That helped a lot. I started producing manuscripts that invited revision instead of aggressively resisting it. One of those later books was a finalist for the Pacific Northwest Writers first-novel contest.

It didn't win, no agent was interested in repping me, and no over-the-transom (look it up) publisher picked it up. That was a painful lesson in humility. But I wasn't tempted to put down the shovel. Despite all the dead ends and rejections, I felt like I was getting somewhere! And I was. So are you, if you keep working.

But here's the point. Writing doesn't get easier; it gets harder. Friends and family may be pulling for you, but only you can keep the iron monster rolling. There will be times when you want to admit defeat, or when you think, after publishing a novel for $5,000 that no one reads, "Is this it?" My oceanography teacher in college wrote a science fiction novel, asked himself that very question, and never wrote another book.

If you're a writer, it's harder *not* to write than it is *to* write. You can quit but you can't hide from your dream, only watch it turn bitter.

Here's the good news. You *own* the train. You can shovel just as hard and as fast as you want. You can make that furnace roar, whatever stage you're at. You can shovel until the iron glows and your hands are blistered, cracked, and bleeding. Nobody can stop you from reaching your potential, if you're determined to get there. How good you are and how close you get to the limits of your talent is one hundred percent in your hands.

So ride that iron monster to the last stop.

Go.

JACK SKILLINGSTEAD's *Harbinger* was nominated for a Locus Award for best first novel. His second novel, *Life on the Preservation*, was a finalist for the Philip K. Dick Award. He has published more than forty short stories to critical acclaim and was short-listed for the Theodore Sturgeon Memorial Award, and his work has been translated internationally.

Congratulations on Learning to Juggle — Now Get on the Unicycle

DARYL GREGORY

I have some bad news and some good news. The bad news (and maybe you've already heard) is that writing is hard — especially, as Thomas Mann pointed out, for writers. The good news is that it's never going to get easier. Really. This is excellent, reassuring news.

It may not seem like it, especially if you're starting out. When I first began writing it was difficult to make *anything* work on the page. Where should the story begin? How do I explain what's going on without boring readers to death? I had trouble moving characters across a room, never mind through a plot. Most of my early stories ended in a shrug — or didn't end at all, because I couldn't finish them. I remember reaching the end of one of my Clarion submission stories practically gasping for air. It was eight pages long.

Once I became able to (most of the time) construct a coherent story, I was alarmed that new and more difficult problems kept raising their heads. The more I wrote, and the more I read as a writer (which is quite a different thing than reading as a civilian), the more aware I became of the distance between what I had done in prose and what others had already accomplished. A few years ago I was reading Geoff Ryman's novel *Air*, and I kept stomping around the living room, shouting to no one, "But how is he *doing* this?"

Writing is not only hard, it's fractally hard. It's difficult at the 30,000-foot level, when you're figuring out the arc of the story. It's tricky at the scene level, when you're trying to make each moment dramatic. And it's painstakingly difficult when you're down amongst the sentences, trying to make every word count. Each story presents a different set of problems, so that the lessons you learned in one novel don't apply to the next.

This continuing, ever-morphing, and escalating difficulty is a sign that you're on the right track. Your job, if you're serious about writing, is not to avoid the hardness, but lean into it. At every opportunity, you need to deliberately make the act of writing even more difficult.

Hear me out.

In the beginning of your career, it's an achievement to merely get the protagonist into trouble and then out of it in a way that keeps readers turning the page. The next level is to resolve your characters' problems in a way that's thematically resonant. Merely solving a puzzle (*Gee, Scoob, Old Man Withers was the ghost the whole time!*) is unengaging unless it's tied to the concerns of the characters. Every story makes a promise that it's the writer's duty to fulfill. If that story is about, say, the difficulty of parents and children communicating, the plot has to resolve with an act of connection, or the failure to connect.

But even if a story keeps its promises, that's still not enough. One of the most difficult things in writing is saying what you mean to say. It's perfectly fine to discover what you think during the writing of a piece (in fact, that's how most writers find out what they think), but after that first draft, you have to interrogate your conclusions. Have you relied on clichés or tired tropes? Are you reflecting the sexism, racism, or classicism in current society, or the attitudes that were baked into the stories you loved as a child? Are you thinking clearly?

When I was a student at Clarion, Samuel R. Delany gave us this suggestion for when we were introducing a character: Don't accept the first candidate for the job that your subconscious shoves forward. Those characters tend to be a lot like you. Instead, see what happens when you "flip" them. Imagine changing a character's gender, socioeconomic status, ethnicity, sexual orientation, country of origin ... everything. See what happens to the story in your head when you make that change.

At Clarion I learned another trick for making my stories more interesting, but this one came from one of my classmates. He wrote a beautiful story in which each scene included the title of a song from a favorite album — in order. Each title was worked into dialogue or mentioned in the prose. It didn't matter that the readers didn't know the album; the track list provided the writer with a scaffold, like a sonnet's rhyme scheme, and that semi-arbitrary constraint pushed his story in less predictable directions.

Since then I've often relied on constraints to shape my own writing. The plot of my first novel echoes the lyrics in David Bowie's "Oh! You Pretty Things." I based a short story on a Johnny Cash cover of a Depeche Mode song. A couple years ago I wrote a story in which the years-long gaps between scenes follow the Fibonacci sequence.

Readers don't need to be aware of any of these influences and architectures to enjoy the piece, and your story can't depend on them for its success. But I have a religious belief that readers can sense the layers beneath the surface, even if they can't identify them, in the way a casual drinker can taste *something* lovely in a whisky without knowing about the charred oak barrel it was aged in.

Often I choose a constraint that targets one of my weaknesses. My first two novels only covered a timespan of weeks, so I decided that my third book would be a David Copperfieldesque story that spanned the protagonist's life from birth to death. (And second death — it was a zombie novel.) Later I realized that all my novels had been either first person or tight third, and I'd avoided the complication of multiple points of view. My next novella was about horror survivors in small group therapy, so I decided that the structure should also follow the therapy process. Each chapter would be that week's session. The "hero" of the story was the group, so each chapter started with "we," before shifting from first-person plural to the point of view of the character telling their story that session. Baroque? Sure. But it fit the theme. I would have had to abandon the structure if it didn't serve the story.

Structure, however, is useless without strong sentences. You can't build a sturdy house out of shoddy timber. Yes, it's a commonplace of science fiction that story trumps prose, and I'm not denying you can make a living building crappy houses — but you don't want to be that person, do you? Be tough on your sentences. I spend hours weeding out subordinate clauses, weak to-be constructions, hackneyed phrases, vague verbs, and superfluous adjectives. I hunt down meaningless gestures and distracting locomotion (all those sentences moving characters in and out of rooms, sipping from coffee cups). Then I add the things I tend to skip in first drafts, such as emotional reactions and interior thoughts. Prose is like cinematography: the audience responds to it even if they don't realize how it works and what it's doing for the story.

Writing is hard, and the writing life is even harder. One night at a con I was complaining to Gardner Dozois, the legendary writer and editor, about how whenever I reached some milestone, I'd be happy for a short time before I became dissatisfied. When I left Clarion, all I wanted was to sell one short story. When that happened, I was elated—for a week. Then I thought, what if that was a fluke? When I sold a second story to that magazine, I was happy for a couple days, and then I thought, what if I can sell only to this one editor? Much later I began to worry that I was unable to sell a novel. Then a second.

At that con, Gardner shook his head and said, "Yeah. Writing is a ladder of sadness." That was true for me. I'd climb a rung, and immediately lament that I hadn't reached the next one—some book deal or movie option or award that those *other people* were getting.

It's fun to whine about publishing with your writer friends—you don't feel like such a solitary loser, but a member of a losing team. But it's also bullshit. I know that if YesterDaryl, that guy who only wanted to sell a single story, heard me complaining about my current woes, he'd travel through time and punch me in the face.

So by all means, celebrate the milestones. But realize that pining for the next one is a trap, because most of those rewards are out of your control. Instead, concentrate on your craft. Take on harder and better problems. There's great satisfaction in creating something beautiful, and joy in knowing you can try again.

DARYL GREGORY's most recent novel is *Spoonbenders*, now in development at Showtime. His other books include five novels, a short story collection, and the novella *We Are All Completely Fine*, which won the World Fantasy and Shirley Jackson awards. Other work has won the Crawford and Dell awards and has been nominated for the Hugo, Nebula, Locus, Sturgeon, and Lambda awards. A novel is forthcoming from Knopf, and Tor.com will be publishing his next novella. He has taught writing—in person!—at various workshops, including Clarion West and Viable Paradise, and hopes to do that again someday.

Writing in the Age of Distraction

CORY DOCTOROW

We know that our readers are distracted and often overwhelmed by the myriad distractions that lie one click away on the internet, but of course, as a writer, you face the same glorious problem: the delirious world of information and communication and community that lurks behind your screen, one alt-tab away from your word processor.

The single worst piece of writing advice I ever got was when Harlan Ellison told me to stay away from the internet because it would only waste my time and wouldn't help my writing. This advice was wrong creatively, professionally, artistically, and personally, but I know where Ellison was coming from. Every now and again, when I see a new website, game, or service, I sense the tug of an attention black hole—a time sink that is just waiting to fill my every discretionary moment with distraction. As a father who writes at least a book per year, half a dozen columns a month, ten or more blog posts a day, plus assorted novellas and stories and speeches, I know just how short time can be and how dangerous distraction is.

But the internet has been very good to me. It's informed my creativity and aesthetics, it's benefited me professionally and personally, and for every moment it steals, it gives back a hundred delights. I'd no sooner give it up than I'd give up fiction or any other pleasurable vice.

I think I've managed to balance things out through a few simple techniques that I've been refining for years. I still sometimes feel frazzled and info-whelmed, but that's rare. Most of the time, I'm on top of my workload and my muse. Here's how I do it:

Adopt a short, regular work schedule. When I'm working on a story or novel, I set a modest daily goal—usually a page or two—and then I meet it every day, *doing nothing else* while I'm working on it. It's not plausible or desirable to try to get the world to go away for hours at a time, but it's entirely possible to make it all shut up for twenty minutes.

Writing a page every day gets me more than a novel per year—do the math—and there's always twenty minutes to be found in a day, no matter what else is going on. Twenty minutes is a short enough interval that it can be claimed from a sleep or meal break (though this shouldn't become a habit).

The secret is to do it every day to keep the momentum going, and to allow your thoughts to wander to your next day's page between sessions. Try to find one or two vivid sensory details to work into the next page, or a *bon mot*, so that you've already got some material when you sit down at the keyboard.

Leave yourself a rough edge. When you hit your daily word goal, **stop**. Stop even if you're in the middle of a sentence. Especially if you're in the middle of a sentence. That way, when you sit down at the keyboard the next day, your first five or ten words are already ordained, so that you get a little push before you begin your work.

Knitters leave a bit of yarn sticking out of the day's knitting so they know where to pick up the next day. Potters leave a rough edge on the wet clay before they wrap it in plastic for the night—it's hard to build on a smooth edge. If you forget to leave yourself a rough edge, delete the last few words you typed the day before and retype them to prime the pump.

Don't research. Researching isn't writing—and vice versa. When you come to a factual matter that you could google in a matter of seconds, *don't*. Don't give in and look up the length of the Brooklyn Bridge, the population of Rhode Island, or the distance to the Sun. That way lies distraction—an endless click trance that will turn your twenty minutes of composing into a half-day's idyll through the web.

Instead, do what journalists do: type "TK" where your fact should go, as in "The Brooklyn Bridge, all TK feet of it, sailed into the air like a kite." The letter pair "TK" appears in very few English words (the one I get tripped up on is "Atkins") so a quick search through your document for "TK" will tell you whether you have any fact-checking to do afterwards. And your editor and copyeditor will recognize it if you miss it and bring it to your attention.

Don't be ceremonious. Forget advice about finding the right atmosphere to coax your muse into the room. Forget candles, music, silence, a good chair, a cigarette, or putting the kids to sleep. It's nice to have all your physical needs met before you write, but if you convince yourself that you can only write in a perfect world, you compound the problem of finding twenty free minutes with the problem of finding the right environment at the same time. When the time is available, just put fingers to keyboard and write. You can put up with noise/silence/kids/discomfort/hunger for twenty minutes.

Kill your word processor. Word, Google Office, and LibreOffice all come with a bewildering array of typesetting and automation options that you can play with forever. Forget it. All that stuff is distraction, and the last thing you want is your tool second-guessing you, "correcting" your spelling, criticizing your sentence structure, and so on.

The programmers who wrote your word processor type all day long, every day, and they have the power to buy or acquire any tool they can imagine for entering text into a computer. They don't write their software with Word. They use a text editor, like vi, Emacs, TextPad, BBEdit, gedit, or any of a host of others. These are some of the most venerable, reliable, powerful tools in the history of software (since they're at the core of all other software), and they have almost no distracting features — but they do have powerful search-and-replace functions. (Best of all, the humble .txt file can be read by practically every application on your computer, can be pasted directly into an email, and can't transmit a virus.)

Real-time communications tools are deadly. The biggest impediment to concentration is your computer's ecosystem of interruption technologies: social media, IM, email alerts, RSS alerts, Skype rings, etc. Anything that requires you to wait for a response, even subconsciously, occupies your attention. Anything that leaps up on your screen to announce something new occupies your attention.

By all means, schedule a chat—voice, text, or video—when it's needed, but leaving your IM running is like sitting down to work after hanging a giant "DISTRACT ME" sign over your desk—one that shines brightly enough to be seen by the entire world. The more you can train your friends and family to use email, message boards, and similar technologies that allow you to save up your conversation for planned sessions instead of demanding your attention *right now*, the better you'll do at carving out those precious twenty minutes.

I don't claim to have invented these techniques, but they're the ones that have made the twenty-first century a good one for me.

CORY DOCTOROW (craphound.com) is a science fiction author, activist, and journalist. He is the author of *Radicalized* and *Walkaway*, science fiction for adults, a YA graphic novel called *In Real Life*, the nonfiction business book *Information Doesn't Want to Be Free*, and young adult novels like *Homeland*, *Pirate Cinema*, and *Little Brother*. His latest books are *Poesy the Monster Slayer*, a picture book for young readers, and *Attack Surface*, an adult sequel to *Little Brother*. He maintains a daily blog at Pluralistic.net. He works for the Electronic Frontier Foundation, is an MIT Media Lab Research Affiliate, is a Visiting Professor of Computer Science at Open University, is a Visiting Professor of Practice at the University of North Carolina's School of Library and Information Science, and co-founded the UK Open Rights Group. Born in Toronto, Canada, he now lives in Los Angeles.

Going Through an Impasse: Evading Writer's Block

EILEEN GUNN

My friend Bob Morales would never admit to being blocked.

"Are you working on something, Bob?" I'd ask.

"I'm going through an impasse," he'd reply, in even, do-not-bug-me tones. Eventually he would emerge from his impasse, having gone over it or under it or around it, and publish a poem, or a single searing comic page, or a revelatory interview with a cultural icon. Even more eventually he produced *The Truth*, an emotionally moving, politically unflinching graphic novel from Marvel, illustrated by the remarkable Kyle Baker. It was worth the wait, and it churned up a good bit of controversy in the comics world. You can google it.

"Writer's block" is often seen as a dreadful disability that can wreck a writer's life, but actually, it's a relatively common experience. I first realized this when I was teaching an informal writing class to sixth-graders. There were about fourteen kids, boys and girls. One of the girls brought her little sister, who was eight, an extremely tiny eight, very tidily dressed, her hair pulled back in a little bun. Very professional-writer-looking, in fact, which was a little scary in an eight-year-old. As we were about to get started, she raised her hand.

"Did you have a question?" I asked. Poor kid. Probably intimidated by all these older kids who already know how to write.

In a tiny but firm voice, she said, "Sometimes when I want to write, I *really* want to write, but I just sit there and I can't think of anything to say."

Eight years old and she had writer's block. I was dumbfounded, so, stalling for time, I asked the rest of the class if they had ever had that experience. Half of them raised their hands.

I thought, "Well, I guess I don't feel so tragically special now," and started the class with a bunch of advice about how to write when you can't.

Although it's a common side-effect of taking your writing seriously, writer's block can become a debilitating emotional state. It's easy to get lost in it, especially if your perception of yourself is closely associated with you being a writer. In this essay, I'll help you analyze the way you experience blocking and offer some suggestions on how to circumvent the trauma and get on with your work.

We can skip the usual discourse about what blocking behavior is, because if you've experienced it, you know what it is, and if you haven't, you don't need my advice right now. We can skip the chat about what causes it, because there are tons of theories, but no answers. (It is so common, however, that I wonder if it has a neurological basis.) And finally, we can skip the noise about how to "cure" it, and go straight to how to deal with it.

If you can't cure writer's block, at least you can learn to write in spite of it, because being blocked doesn't mean you're doing writing wrong. Maybe that's just how you do it, and maybe you can learn to do it differently.

The first step is to spend a little time thinking. Here are a few questions to ask yourself about the way you personally experience writer's block. This is not a quiz: it's more an inventory. There's nothing to get wrong, and you don't need to show it to anyone. Respond to each question separately. Write down your responses, and say as much or as little as you want.

- What happens when you're feeling blocked?
- What starts the block?
- How do you actually feel when you are blocking?
- What do you think causes it?
- How do you get out of the block?
- What is the worst thing that could happen if you finish the story?

The emotional effects of blocking can be similar to Elisabeth Kübler-Ross's stages of grief. It's useful to identify and examine your feelings and how you deal with them. Ask yourself these questions, and write down your responses. If the question doesn't resonate with you, just write *that* down.

- When you're blocked, do you deny that it's happening to you? (I'm not blocked. I just need to build a birdhouse.)
- Do you get angry at yourself? (I get so mad at myself for not being able to write.)
- Do you get angry at someone else? (My English teacher screwed me up so bad, I'll never be able to write.)
- Do you bargain with the block? (Okay, if I wash the kitchen floor, can I count that as my writing goal for today? The floor's really dirty.... .)
- Are you sad? Do you feel depressed or helpless?
- Can you accept feeling blocked? (This is just the way my mind works.) Sometimes acceptance can help you relax and recognize that these feelings of frustration are just an ordinary part of your writing process, not some special event that you need to panic about.
- Is there some meaning in all of this? Do you have some clues as to how your blocking might relate to other events in your life—immediately, or in a larger perspective?

Try to figure out how you feel about your blocking behavior. Does it have a positive aspect? Does it allow you to do something that you want to do, or avoid something that you don't? Is there some other way to resolve that issue?

The goal here is to acknowledge your feelings. Examine your emotions, then figure out how to make them work for you. Don't ignore or repress them, because having these emotions could be an important part of your writing process. Try to find emotional balance when writing, and to replace any feelings of loss of control with a sense of being in charge. You are the boss of your block: you can figure out how to deal with it.

In any case, give yourself a break. Don't agonize. It's not a moral failing to be a slow writer, nor is it a virtue. It does not necessarily make someone a better writer to agonize over every word. The best time to agonize over words is after they're written—but before they're published.

In addition to looking at emotional issues, there are many useful strategies for disrupting the process of blocking.

Move away from the block. Edit some previous writing. Turn your attention to a different scene. Or just let go of what you can't control, and eliminate a scene that's giving you trouble from the story. Do you really need it? You can always go back later and put it in.

Or just write the block into the story, if you're planning a scene in which a protagonist feels frustrated or miserable. You can acknowledge your feelings and write them into the story.

Give your writing brain a rest and engage your creativity. Try disconnecting from words. Draw pictures and make diagrams about your story.

Step away from the computer. Write in long-hand on actual pieces of paper. (Retro, but it works.)

Go for a walk or a bike ride. Take a notebook, but stop thinking about your story. Notice something you never noticed before. It doesn't have to be something spectacular. A rock, a tree, a fence. Pay attention to it, take notes. Later, write the object you saw into your story.

Go to a museum. Take a notebook. Find an interesting object in a part of the museum you never go into. Spend some time with it. Draw the object.

Watch a movie, go to a concert. Got that notebook with you? Let your mind wander, and write down any ideas that come to you while your brain is off duty.

Put the problem part aside; work on another part. A few days later, go back to the part that's giving you trouble. Work your way back into it, adding details: scents, sounds, whatever.

Set a deadline that you don't control. Volunteer to read a new story online or at a bookstore or a convention. Volunteer for an anthology, enter a contest, make a public proclamation, or do anything else that gives you a deadline. Make a commitment that you will have something done. When the deadline comes, what you have is it. It's done.

However, do not set deadlines you can't meet, and especially don't do that with publishers. There's a reason they're called deadlines.

Become a creature of habit. Make a recurring appointment with your writing self—daily, weekly, monthly, whatever works in your no-doubt complicated life. And then keep the appointment. Wake up early, stay up late, write on your lunch hour, whatever.

Sometimes it helps you keep the appointment if you involve another person. Meet on Zoom to write together. Go to a favorite café or pub.

This habit thing is especially difficult for me, as I am happiest in the middle of chaos, but when I have been able to do it, it has worked really well. During the pandemic, I am meeting with others to write in two-hour Zoom sessions two or three times a day, and I have been very productive.

Create a writing cave. Ideally, every writer would have a private space just to write in. But most people don't. If constant interruptions keep you from writing, claim a space that can be yours, even if it's just a corner of the sofa. Pick a time when your responsibilities are least, and tell people not to bother you. Be assertive. ("Not now. This is my writing time.") Lock yourself in a closet, if that's the only place you can work uninterrupted. Jessica Amanda Salmonson wrote the entire Tomoe Gozen trilogy in a closet.

Set goals and give yourself a reward when you meet them. Did you meet a goal? You get a cookie, a movie, a tour of Antarctica, whatever makes you feel rewarded. For me, the reward is getting something done.

Worried about getting ideas? Relax: everything is an idea. You are surrounded by starting points for ideas.

Pick up a dictionary. Turn to a page at random, and without looking, just stab at the page. Write down the word your finger is on. Do this again with another part of the dictionary. Put those two words together, and see if they spark an idea for a story. If they don't, just relax and do it again. This is how Vonda McIntyre got the idea for *Dreamsnake*.

Pull a character out of a painting, sculpture, other work of art, or even just a random magazine ad. Don't describe the art, just the character. Describe their mood. Put them in your story, or build a story around them.

In the beginning, think small. Listen to Linus Torvalds, who created the Linux operating system, a huge 30-year co-operative project: "Nobody should start to undertake a large project. You start with a small trivial project, and you should never expect it to get large. If you do, you'll just overdesign and generally think it is more important than it likely is at that stage. Or worse, you might be scared away by the sheer size of the work you envision. So start small, and think about the details. Don't think about some big picture and fancy design."

Set yourself an easily achievable goal. Write 500 words nonstop. The goal is simply to get words on paper. They don't have to be about the topic you're blocked on. They don't have to be spelled correctly or punctuated at all. All words count, even the same word typed over and over, but you can't cut and paste. Individually hand-typed words only!

Or write nonstop for fifteen minutes. The goal is to write without censoring yourself. Write anything that comes into your head, even the same word over and over.

When I do this, I find that after writing the same word a hundred times, boredom defeats writer's block, and I actually start a new scene or a new story.

Come at the story from a new direction. Add something from out of left field that has nothing to do with the story line. Then ask yourself, once this detail is introduced, what it might have to do with the rest of the story. Australian writer McKinley Valentine suggests grabbing a random book, opening it at random, and choosing an object or idea from it to put into the next scene of your story.

Is the middle of the story giving you problems? This seems to be the part of a writing project that troubles everybody at some point. There's no one solution, but there are a lot of things to try.

Start from the end and work back to the middle. Write the ending scene. Write the one before it, and the one before that. Eventually, you'll get to the beginning, and then you have something to edit.

Or make the project smaller: break it up. Divide the middle up by characters, by setting, by action. Work out each separately, then put them together.

Move away from words and draw diagrams. Diagram rising and falling action. Diagram set pieces, if you have them (where action is predictable to you). Set pieces can be self-contained units of action or exciting scenes that are integral to the plot. Diagram everything that moves or changes. Draw charts or diagrams for all the plot threads, for all the principle characters, even for all the settings. Do the beginning, do the endings, and then connect them in the middle.

Or stop thinking about the big picture. Make something immediate happen to your protagonist, even if it seems dumb at the moment. Trust that your subconscious will give you something that you can make better, and finesse it later.

Divide your story into acts, like a play. Try three acts or five acts. This should help you understand the larger structure of how tension in the plot rises and falls. Then you have a one-act or three-act middle to deal with, and you can break each act into scenes. You might not know what's in each of the scenes, but you'll have a better understanding of the pacing and how the parts relate to one another.

Writing a long and complex story, it's easy to get lost in the middle, especially if you're the kind of writer, as I am, who doesn't map everything out in advance. In such a situation you may have lost track of the motivations or subplots. One way to resolve that is to ask one of the minor characters what's going on. Sometimes your lesser characters have been paying attention while you're focused on the protagonist. You don't have to put it in the story, but you might learn something useful.

Have you lost track of a complex plot? Try using Scrivener. Scrivener is a modestly priced word-processing program made for outlining, organizing, and re-organizing a story or novel. I think of it as a structural-planning tool, rather than a word-processing tool, and I use my regular word-processing program for pulling everything together into a final draft.

Scrivener can be very helpful for drafting a complex story, for untangling the middle, or for understanding how the pieces of your story fit together. It makes it easier to notice where there are gaps in a narrative, and to move around from one part to another, which is useful if you're blocking on one part. The very act of moving your document to Scrivener can help you understand your own work better, and may help you work out plot issues that have eluded you. You can download it and try it out for free, and they have friendly support techs. Google it.

Are you agonizing over the end of a story? If you feel blocked because you are trying to work out the ending, don't try to get there via the story. Step back from the story and ask yourself how it all ends. Your subconscious may know perfectly well what to do. Some writers even write the ending first. Ted Chiang does.

Got a problem with a finished work? Maybe your story is technically "finished," but you don't feel it's done yet: you have a generalized dissatisfaction with it. Time to play rough with the work you've created.

Play safely. Put a printout in a file drawer and put a digital file in a separate directory. Now your story is safe. It's fine. Nothing you do can hurt it.

Then make a copy of it. This is just a copy: your real story is safe elsewhere. Now you can tear into it: change things, move things around, make new connections. Cut it into strips and shuffle them, William-Burroughs-style. Put the changed text aside for a day or two, then look and see what you've got. It might be better than the copy in the safe place. But if it's not, no problem.

Partner with your subconscious. This can be a huge help with writing difficulties. Approach your subconscious with respect, and define the problem well when asking it for help.

Try putting your mind to work while you're asleep. First define the problem and write it down. Then write down specific questions about the story.

Put a notebook and pen by your bed. Then, before you go to sleep, think about the problem and questions you've defined, and tell your subconscious that you want it to work this out while you're asleep. (Be nice! Your subconscious doesn't like to be ordered around.) When you wake up, check in with it again and write down anything that occurs to you. Don't censor yourself or criticize your thoughts: just write them down. Then follow your usual routine, and trust that when you sit down to write, words will come and this block will be broken. Sometimes this works, and sometimes it doesn't, but give it a try: you're going to go to sleep tonight anyway, right?

Sometimes it's helpful to use the *I Ching*, the tarot, or similar traditional methods to clarify a problem you're having and point you towards a solution. This can relate to the block you're experiencing or to a plotting problem that's giving you pause. It's generally useful to frame a specific question, such as "How do I get past this block?" or "Should Frodo throw the Ring into Mount Doom or keep it for himself?"

Think about the question as you do the ritual, or as someone does it for you. If you haven't used these methods before, get some guidance when using them the first time, either by reading about them, or having a more experienced friend walk you through them.

The *I Ching* (I use the Wilhelm/Baynes translation) especially likes specific questions, and it tends to give specific advice, though sometimes you'll need to interpret it. Carl Jung's essay on the *I Ching*, while problematic in his discussion of Chinese science, approaches the book and the human subconscious with respect: https://www.iging.com/intro/foreword.htm. Jung's advice is to treat the book as you would a wise elder that you are consulting.

I recommend using the yarrow-stalk divination method, rather than tossing coins, because it takes about twenty minutes to sort the stalks, and that gives your subconscious some time to work on your problem. The coin method is faster; there is a minor mathematical difference in the results, but it doesn't affect the main reading. For a good online guide to the *I Ching*, try I Ching Online, which will even toss the coins for you: https://www.ichingonline.net/.

The tarot is also a way of examining your subconscious. Get a tarot card reading, or do one for yourself. Tarot cards can offer psychological insight into characters and plot events, and even into your blocking behavior.

Now make your own list of strategies. There are no rules. What works for me will not necessarily work for you, and what works today might not work tomorrow. Take some time to explore different strategies. Figure out what works best to keep you writing, and line up some alternatives if that stops working at some point.

Life is too short to stop writing just because you're blocked, so don't beat yourself up about it. Treat it as a temporary state that you can get yourself out of, or simply incorporate it into your writing process and keep working.

Go to it! Make your way through that impasse—over it, under it, or around it—get to the other side, and get on with your work. You can do it.

EILEEN GUNN is the author of two story collections: *Questionable Practices* (Small Beer Press, 2014) and *Stable Strategies and Others* (Tachyon Publications, 2004). Her fiction has received the Nebula Award in the US and the Sense of Gender Award in Japan, and has been nominated for the Hugo, Philip K. Dick, and World Fantasy awards and short-listed for the James Tiptree, Jr. award. She wrote all of it while blocked.

On Mentors and Mentees

CAT RAMBO

One of the great traditions in fantasy and science fiction writing is that of the mentor/mentee relationship. We're told of many of the earlier writers mentoring newer ones: offering advice, passing along opportunities, and sometimes collaborating. The Science Fiction and Fantasy Writers of America (SFWA) arose out of that impulse to help fellow writers and acknowledge that helping others was one of the best ways to help the industry overall.

I first became aware of the tradition in a workshop with Ann Crispin, who was one of the great mentors, teaching and guiding countless writers, and I've always been glad I followed her advice. Gazing out over a basement room full of DragonCon writers, she solemnly told us: "Here's what you do. You sell a story at SFWA pro rates. You join SFWA. And you start paying it forward then."

Sometimes this relationship takes the form of collaborating with newer writers. I was lucky enough to do so with Jeff VanderMeer on a novelette called "The Surgeon's Tale," and many of the things I learned while working on that piece remain with me to this day. Mike Resnick was another writer known for mentoring younger ones, collaborating with literally dozens of them, and I myself wrote a story with Mike, "The Mermaid Club," in which we had a lot of fun spoofing Starbucks. You always learn something when you work with another writer, and it is particularly illuminating to work with someone who really knows their stuff.

But knowing of this tradition's existence can frustrate a new writer, particularly one that is geographically separated from their fellow writers, and make them feel as though they are missing out on one of the more important advantages. At the same time, there is a certain wistful mystique that sometimes distorts what the relationship actually is, and that's understandable: who doesn't want someone older and wiser who wants to help you succeed and open opportunities to you? The truth is, that rarely, if ever, happens.

How do you find mentors? There are several traditional ways.

Go where the writers are. Nowadays there are virtual spaces open for networking: discussion boards and Discord channels, online conferences, and other gatherings. Go and spend some time connecting with people. Volunteering is one of the best ways to become part of a community in a way that will help you identify who may be willing to act as a mentor.

Figure out who the *mentorly* types are. Look for the writers who spend time promoting other people, who recommend other people's works—not just their own. Watch them on panels to see who gracefully encourages other voices to speak and listens to them when they do. Look for the people who are trying to do things right.

SFWA. SFWA created and runs a program that connects mentors and mentees, but the program is only open at certain times of the year. Check the SFWA website (sfwa.org) for details. You do not need to be a member to be a mentee or a mentor.

Take workshops and classes. Afterward, let the instructors know about what you're doing. I'm always pleased when a student tells me that something written in class has found a home, and many of my mentees come from the pool of those that have taken my classes.

Don't ask. Should you mail someone out of the blue and say, "Be my mentor?" In my experience, probably not, unless you have some definite tie with them to which you can point. Being too aggressive at this point actually is a way to get yourself known—but not in a good way.

A mentoring relationship is, in my experience, something that grows slowly, sometimes perhaps out of some small ask or perhaps from a shared experience like a workshop or panel at a convention. It's definitely a form of friendship, but it's one that, to me at least, seems to be one that pulls from the teacher/student relationship as well, and as such has all the same needs for ethical behavior that one would expect out of the latter.

This is important to stress, for two reasons. One, human beings are human beings and sometimes attracted to each other in a way where they act first and think afterward. Sex skews the power dynamic. The two relationships cannot co-exist without affecting each other in a way that is, in my opinion, negative.

Two, as with any industry, there are predators. If someone offers to mentor you in some capacity, whether it is formal or informal, and it comes with romantic expectations, this is unacceptable. Be aware that it often begins with small jokes or flirtatious gestures—if a mentor is making you uncomfortable, I suggest severing the relationship. You may want to talk to other people who are being mentored by them. You can also contact SFWA's Writer Beware program so they are aware of the behavior at writerbeware@sfwa.org.

If you have someone you can think of as a mentor, keep some things in mind when dealing with them. Your mentor has their own career, their own work, their own ambitions, their own frustrations and fears. In short, they are as human as you, even if you admire their writing. Make sure they understand that you know and appreciate their efforts on your behalf, and that includes being willing to give you chunks of time in a world where that resource is usually the most scarce of all.

Here are some other things to keep in mind:

Keep working on your own behalf. Use your mentor to assist with that; don't think it will be the other way around. If you're not putting in effort, why should they?

Be responsive in a timely way. Don't ghost people—or if you think you are likely to, let them know what's going to happen beforehand. I'm more tolerant of a little flakiness on the part of someone who tells me ahead of time that they have issues with depression than otherwise. Let them know what you're doing, and share some of the joys when they occur.

Pay attention to your mentor's advice and follow it. Or else have a decent explanation why you didn't. It's okay to evaluate advice and not take it, but that's different than not listening in the first place.

Don't treat them like a therapist. There's a reason therapists charge money, and part of it is that listening to other people talk at length about their problems can be very draining.

Treat them well. Treat your mentor, rather, like a respected friend, whose opinion you value.

Don't expect a mentor to beta read, critique, or copyedit your work. That's unrealistic and will only lead to disappointment.

Do not ask them to introduce you to their agent. If that's likely to happen, they will make the offer.

Volunteer. Volunteer for things. Help where you can, because it's never too early to start developing that ethic.

If you become a mentor yourself, try to keep in mind that mentoring people who are unlike you will often be the most rewarding experience, and that they will be the ones from whom you learn the most. Actively trying to find mentees who are unlike you also helps fight the human tendency to be drawn to those we physically resemble, a tendency that perpetuates existing power structures such as racism, ableism, transphobia and other negative tendencies.

This is, in fact, one of the best ways to make sure that our field continues to grow in diversity. Perhaps not coincidentally, it's an excellent way to grow as a writer and a teacher yourself.

CAT RAMBO lives, writes, and teaches somewhere in the Pacific Northwest. Their 200+ fiction publications include stories in *Asimov's*, *Clarkesworld* magazine, and *The Magazine of Fantasy and Science Fiction*. Their most recent works are Nebula Award winner *Carpe Glitter* (Meerkat Press) and *And the Last Trump Shall Sound* (co-written with James Morrow and Harry Turtledove, Arc Manor). Forthcoming are fantasy novel *Exiles of Tabat* (Wordfire Press, spring 2021) and space opera *You Sexy Thing* (Tor Macmillan, 2021). Rambo is a 2005 Clarion West graduate.

Pitfalls of Writing Science Fiction & Fantasy: General Useful Information & Other Opinionated Comments

VONDA N. MCINTYRE

Read This First!
McIntyre's First Law:
Under the right circumstances, anything I tell you could be wrong.

Pitfall #1: The expository lump, or, "As you know, George, the space station's orbit is degrading rapidly, and we're running out of air."

Every SF story contains information that the reader must know. Getting that information across gracefully is difficult, but rewarding. Handing it to the reader in the narrative can be done carefully. Handing it to the reader in a lump of expository dialogue is generally not graceful.

Detection trick: If the phrase "As you know" or "As you should know" would make sense in a line of dialogue, the dialogue is probably an expository lump.

Under no circumstances (except for broad humor) should you insert the phrase "As you know" into a line of dialogue, even if it would make sense. Especially if it would make sense! If the only way to get information to the reader (after you've sweated trying to get it in some other way) is by having one character tell it to another who already knows it, for heaven's sake don't draw attention to the fact by adding "as you know."

Useful technique: It's easier to describe something if it's broken. If something is broken, then you *notice* it. If it's working right, it just sits there being invisible doing its job. Not to be overused!

Pitfall #2: It's almost writing, or, Half-baked weasels

Almost and *half* (half-smile, etc.) are **weasel words** that allow you to evade the responsibility of being precise. Their use will drain the life from your prose. "Some kind of" has recently joined the infamous company of weasel words. If you're tempted to use this phrase, ask yourself what meaning it conveys. That the writer has no idea what's going on? That the writer knows but isn't going to bother to tell the reader? It carries no information. Why use it? Some writers litter their pages with these words and phrases to no purpose. Beware!

Pitfall #3: Subjunctive tension, or, "Don't mince words, Bones, tell me what you really mean!"

Samuel R. Delany coined the term **subjunctive tension,** which is the difference between what you mean and what you actually say. In "realistic" fiction you can get away with a lot of metaphorical (not to say sloppy) phrasings that, in science fiction, can bring the reader up short.

Examples:
His eyes fell to the floor.
(Boing! Boing!)
She screwed up her face.
(To the ceiling? Owie!)
He ran through the door.
(Able to penetrate strong oak in a single bound! Might one possibly mean the doorway?)
She strained her eyes through the viewscreen.
(My all-time fave.)

Pitfall #4: Rampant capitals, or, The Nouns of Doom

Be careful about capitalizing words in order to indicate their importance. Several problems attend *rampant capitalization.*

First, extraneous capitalization tries and fails to conceal a lack of intensity, style, substance, or all those qualities, in your prose.

Second, if you capitalize Many of the Nouns in your Sentences, your Prose your Wish a Story in German to write will read. (In German you capitalize all the nouns.) (And the verbs come last, but that's a different Pitfall.)

Third, when you sell your novel, the cover blurb will contain every single word you've capitalized. Here is a possible result:

On the Plains of Mystery, Prince Greeb of the Empire of Thorns rides his WindHorse, Fred, to challenge the TrollBugs to a FireDuel!

You get my drift. It looks dumb. Don't set yourself up for it.

Pitfall #5: Species vs. specie, or, How much for just that species?

A **species** is a group of living things reproductively isolated from other groups. The plural of species is species. **Specie** means money, specifically, coined money.

Other false singulars: Phenomena is plural; its singular is phenomenon. Series is both singular and plural; the singular is not serie. Bacterium is the singular; bacteria is the plural. Criterion: singular; criteria: plural. Biceps is the singular. Bicepses is the plural, though you can use biceps if you insist. There is no such thing as a bicep. Or a tricep. Or a quadricep.

The human species is *Homo sapiens*. An individual human is still *Homo sapiens*, not *Homo sapien*.

Pitfall #6: Ygdylc'haafuk's revenge, or, McIntyre's Laws of Titles

Never use a title that is **impossible to pronounce** or **embarrassing to say.**

Doing either causes people to find it awkward to discuss your book. For example, *Superluminal* (a book of mine) has been misspelled and mispronounced by everybody, up to and including the *New York Times* ("... her novel *Superliminal*, which she says means 'faster than light.' ")

Pitfall #7: Neologisms, or, Calling a rabbit a smeerp, or, This essay almost made my spell-checker toss its cookies

Neologisms are made-up words. Be very careful with them. If you're good at them, terrific. (Heinlein was great at them. I got all the way through *The Moon is a Harsh Mistress* before I realized that *tanstaafl* wasn't a perfectly good Dutch word, and I used to live in the Netherlands.)

If you aren't good at them, you can make yourself sound silly.

In particular, watch out for what Damon Knight called "calling a rabbit a smeerp." Just because you call a long-eared, short-tailed lagomorphic mammal with long hind legs a "smeerp," that doesn't make it alien.

We all write SF in standard English, unless we are Anthony Burgess (who did made-up dialect well), or some other people who do it not so well. There's no particular reason to translate words for time, distance, and food into gibberish. (I don't know why time, distance, and food are so susceptible to this in science fiction, but they are.) If your characters are drinking coffee, have them drink coffee, not "klaa" or "jav." Coffee's been around for more than a millennium. It's probably going to last.

Besides, as a linguistically oriented friend of mine pointed out with some exasperation, almost all the made-up words in science fiction written by English speakers sound like made-up words derived from English.

Pitfall #8: It looks like seem or appear! or, These seem to be more weasels

Be *very* careful about the use of words such as "seem" and "appear," especially in science fiction. As Samuel R. Delany pointed out, in SF things can happen that are unlikely to happen in real life or in realistic ("mainstream") fiction. Therefore, if you *use* "seem," you should *mean* "seem." As in, "This is what it looked like but this *isn't really what's going on, so pay attention!*"

A perceptive reader will note "seem" or "appear" or "looked like," perk up their ears, and wait for you to tell them what really is going on. If nothing other than the superficial action is going on, the reader is going to be irritated.

Eventually the reader will quit trusting you.

Pitfall #9: Department of Redundancy Department, or, Department of Redundancy Department

Samuel R. Delany's technique for determining whether a phrase is redundant (if **you** have any question): choose one of the words you suspect of being redundant. Switch it to its antonym. If the resulting construction is inherently ridiculous, an oxymoron, you have redundancy. For example, a "large giant." As opposed to a small giant? Other common speech-habit redundancies include the rich heiress and the consensus of opinion.

Hyperbole is a fine and respected literary tradition, and speech habits are indispensable for creating characters. (Think of Stephen Maturin's charming habit of saying "little small.")

But when you use these techniques, be sure you know you're doing it—and why.

Pitfall #10: An activity almost like writing, or, Something resembling weasels

A current curious fad among writers who should know better is the construction "[Character] felt something like [emotion]." Example: "He felt something like annoyance." Extreme example: "She felt something almost like amusement." Over-the-top example: "He felt something vaguely approaching absurdity."

One possible explanation for avoiding accurate description is that the writer doesn't know what the character is experiencing, and can't take the trouble to figure it out.

In some cases, the writer has grasped at a metaphor and clutched an illusion.

When I encounter this construction, I'm always left with the impression that the character (or more likely, the writer) has such refined sensibilities and lofty feelings that I, the lowly reader, can't be expected to comprehend them ... so why should the writer bother trying to describe them?

And why should I bother trying to read them?

Pitfall #11: Literal vs. figurative, or, "His head literally ... exploded!"

"Figuratively" means that you are speaking metaphorically or symbolically. "Literally" means that you are speaking with precision and realism, that you are saying what exactly happened. "Literally" is not a generic intensifier. If you are talking about someone's headache, "figuratively exploded" is the phrase you're looking for—at least in comparison to "literally exploded."

Pitfall #12: "I am an amateur," or, Seven ways to get your manuscript rejected

1. Turn Page 100 upside-down or surreptitiously dog-ear pages 8 and 9 together to be sure the editor has read the whole typescript. (All editors have seen these tricks; some find them so insulting that they'll leave the pages turned upside down or dog-eared even if they have read that far.)

2. Beg the editor to buy your story so you can pay for your mother's operation.

3. Track down the editor's email address and email your manuscript, even though the publication's guidelines ask you not to.

4. Send an editor hate mail to inform them how stupid they are for having rejected your story. Quibble with every comment they took the time to make. This is a fine technique for getting future manuscripts rejected.

5. Ostentatiously display a copyright © notice (on *every single page!*) so the editor will know not to steal your ideas. (Ideas are easy, and parallel evolution of story lines is common. It's what you do with the ideas that counts.)

6. Warn the editor outright not to steal your ideas, because you have (or are) a hotshot lawyer. (See #5. Plagiarism does happen, but it's rare—editors have not, to my knowledge, been the perpetrators—and it *always* blows up in the plagiarist's face. Editors aren't interested in stealing anyone's stories to make themselves look good. What makes editors look good is finding writers who can write good stories, and publishing them.)

7. Send a nonstandard manuscript "so it will stand out." Pink paper with purple type. Perfect-bound camera-ready manuscripts. Typeset text. If the editor sends you information on proper manuscript format—by all means, argue with the old fuddy-duddy.

Pitfall #13: Size matters! er... Doesn't it?

A word that is similar to another word, but longer, is not necessarily an intensified version of the shorter word. For example, "penultimate" does not mean the absolutely completely most important pinnacle, the ultimate of ultimates.

Nor is it an esoteric sexual technique.

It means "next to last."

Similarly, a center is a single point. It's hard to imagine something more precise than a single point, and yet writers and commentators will try to emphasize the focus of an event by calling it the "epicenter."

(Some experts approve of using "epicenter" this way. I'm holding out for using it only to refer to the place on the earth's surface above the focus of an earthquake.)

"Enormity," "problematic," and "singular" are other words commonly misused. If you don't know what they mean, look them up. If you aren't certain what a word means, look it up.

Every so often, look up a word you think you know the meaning of. You might be surprised. (I sometimes am.)

President Obama used both enormity and singular correctly in his election night speech. (He can also pronounce "nuclear.")

There's hope for us yet.

Pitfall #14: Everything's in the right place! or, If it were somewhere else, that would be something to mention

A current pet peeve of mine is the ordinary event described as if it were extraordinary, because the situation is extraordinary. My hypothesis is that the writer overwrites the event under the misapprehension that excess results in intensity.

His heart beat in his chest. Where else, ordinarily, would your heart beat? Your chest is where your heart is supposed to be. If you can feel it beating elsewhere, if it's beating so hard you can hear your own pulse, if you're seriously injured and you can see the pulse in the flow of blood, that's worth mentioning.

I thought to myself. Who else, ordinarily, would you think to? I can imagine writing a story about telepathy in which thinking to myself might be a challenge, but I can't think of any other time when I'd need to mention that it was me I was thinking to.

She took off the cap on her head. Where else would you keep your cap but on your head? If your character is wearing it someplace else, you might want to point that out. It could tell the reader something important about the character. Otherwise, just take off the cap already. If you're being paid by the word, think of some better words to get paid for.

The taste of cold iron in his mouth. Taste is something that happens in your mouth. If you taste something, it's going to be your tongue that tastes it. Have you ever experienced tasting something that wasn't in your mouth? It's not that uncommon; one effect of some chemicals (DMSO, for example) when they're applied to your skin is that you can taste them. Where you taste them is in your mouth. If you taste them somewhere else, you've got something interesting going on. (You can't have that idea; I'm using it.)

She looked down at the ground by her feet. I particularly like this one. It's a threefer. You convey the same information with "She looked down," "She looked at the ground," and "She looked at her feet." If she looks down and she doesn't see either the ground or her feet, you may have some explaining to do.

I was reading a novel the other day and encountered three overwritten and redundant phrases in one paragraph. This was one of the reasons I eventually gave up reading the book.

On the other hand, the novel was by a writer who regularly shows up on the bestseller list, so what do I know? Maybe we all should write using multiple redundancies.

VONDA N. MCINTYRE (1948–2019) was not only the godmother of the Clarion West Writers Workshop, but the multi-nominated author of many novels, including *The Exile Waiting*, *Superluminal*, *The Bride*, and the Starfarers Quartet series, as well as the short fiction collection *Fireflood and Other Stories*. She wrote novels in the Star Trek universe, including *Enterprise: The First Adventure* and *The Entropy Effect*, and the novelizations of the films *Star Trek II: The Wrath of Khan*, *Star Trek III: The Search for Spock*, and *Star Trek IV: The Voyage Home*. She also wrote a Star Wars novel, *The Crystal Star*. She attended the Clarion Workshop in 1970, and in 1971 founded the Clarion West Writers Workshop. In 1973, she won the Nebula Award for her novelette "Of Mist, and Grass and Sand," which formed the basis of her novel *Dreamsnake*, which in turn won both the Hugo and Nebula Awards. *The Moon and the Sun* won the Nebula Award in 1997 and was later adapted into an unreleased feature film, *The King's Daughter*.

Positive Obsession

OCTAVIA E. BUTLER

1. My mother read me bedtime stories until I was six years old. It was a sneak attack on her part. As soon as I really got to like the stories, she said, "Here's the book. Now you read." She didn't know what she was setting us both up for.

2. "I think," my mother said to me one day when I was ten, "that everyone has something that they can do better than they can do anything else. It's up to them to find out what that something is."

We were in the kitchen by the stove. She was pressing my hair while I sat bent over someone's cast-off notebook, writing. I had decided to write down some of the stories I'd been telling myself over the years. When I didn't have stories to read, I learned to make them up. Now I was learning to write them down.

3. I was shy, afraid of most people, most situations. I didn't stop to ask myself how things could hurt me, or even whether they could hurt me. I was just afraid.

I crept into my first bookstore full of vague fears. I had managed to save about five dollars, mostly in change. It was 1957. Five dollars was a lot of money for a ten-year-old. The public library had been my second home since I was six, and I owned a number of hand-me-down books. But now I wanted a new book—one I had chosen, one I could keep.

"Can kids come in here?" I asked the woman at the cash register once I was inside. I meant could Black kids come in. My mother, born in rural Louisiana and raised amid strict racial segregation, had warned me that I might not be welcome everywhere, even in California.

The cashier glanced at me. "Of course you can come in," she said. Then, as though it were an afterthought, she smiled. I relaxed.

The first book I bought described the characteristics of different breeds of horses. The second described stars and planets, asteroids, moons, and comets.

4. My aunt and I were in her kitchen, talking. She was cooking something that smelled good, and I was sitting at her table, watching. Luxury. At home, my mother would have had me helping.

"I want to be a writer when I grow up," I said.

"Do you?" my aunt asked. "Well that's nice, but you'll have to get a job, too."

"Writing will be my job," I said.

"You can write any time. It's a nice hobby. But you'll have to earn a living."

"As a writer."

"Don't be silly."

"I mean it."

"Honey ... Negroes can't be writers."

"Why not?"

"They just can't."

"Yes, they can, too!"

I was most adamant when I didn't know what I was talking out. In all my thirteen years, I had never read a printed word that I knew to have been written by a Black person. My aunt was a grown woman. She knew more than I did. What if she were right?

5. Shyness is shit.

It isn't cute or feminine or appealing. It's torment, and it's shit.

I spent a lot of my childhood and adolescence staring at the ground. It's a wonder I didn't become a geologist. I whispered. People were always saying, "Speak up! We can't hear you."

I memorized required reports and poems for school, then cried my way out of having to recite. Some teachers condemned me for not studying. Some forgave me for not being very bright. Only a few saw my shyness.

"She's so backward," some of my relatives said.

"She's so nice and quiet," tactful friends of my mother said.

I believed I was ugly and stupid, clumsy, and socially hopeless. I also thought that everyone would notice these faults if I drew attention to myself. I wanted to disappear. Instead, I grew to be six feet tall. Boys in particular seemed to assume that I had done this growing deliberately and that I should be ridiculed for it as often as possible.

I hid out in a big pink notebook—one that would hold a whole ream of paper. I made myself a universe in it. There I could be a magic horse, a Martian, a telepath. ... There I could be anywhere but here, any time but now, with any people but these.

6. My mother did day work. She had a habit of bringing home any books her employers threw out. She had been permitted only three years of school. Then she had been put to work. Oldest daughter. She believed passionately in books and education. She wanted me to have what she had been denied. She wasn't sure which books I might be able to use, so she brought whatever she found in the trash. I had books yellow with age, books without covers, books written in, crayoned in, spilled on, cut, torn, even partly burned. I stacked them in wooden crates and secondhand bookcases and read them when I was ready for them. Some were years too advanced for me when I got them, but I grew into them.

7. An obsession, according to my old Random House dictionary, is "the domination of one's thoughts or feelings by a persistent idea, image, desire, etc." Obsession can be a useful tool if it's positive obsession. Using it is like aiming carefully in archery.

I took archery in high school because it wasn't a team sport. I liked some of the team sports, but in archery you did well or badly according to your own efforts. No one else to blame. I wanted to see what I could do. I learned to aim high. Aim above the target. Aim just *there!* Relax. Let go. If you aimed right, you hit the bull's-eye. I saw positive obsession as a way of aiming yourself, your life, at your chosen target. Decide what you want. Aim high. Go for it.

I wanted to sell a story. Before I knew how to type, I wanted to sell a story.

I pecked my stories out two fingered on the Remington portable typewriter my mother had bought me. I had begged for it when I was ten, and she had bought it.

"You'll spoil that child!" one of her friends told her. "What does she need with a typewriter at her age? It will soon be sitting in the closet with dust on it. All that money wasted!"

I asked my science teacher, Mr. Pfaff, to type one of my stories for me—type it the way it was supposed to be with no holes erased into the paper and no strikeovers. He did. He even corrected my terrible spelling and punctuation. To this day I'm amazed and grateful.

8. I had no idea how to submit a story for publication. I blundered through unhelpful library books on writing. Then I found a discarded copy of *The Writer*, a magazine I had never heard of. That copy sent me back to the library to look for more, and for other writers' magazines to see what I could learn from them. In very little time I'd found out how to submit a story, and my story was in the mail. A few weeks later I got my first rejection slip.

When I was older, I decided that getting a rejection slip was like being told your child was ugly. You got mad and didn't believe a word of it. Besides, look at all the really ugly literary children out there in the world being published and doing fine!

9. I spent my teens and much more of my twenties collecting printed rejections. Early on, my mother lost $61.20—a reading fee charged by a so-called agent to look at one of my unpublishable stories. No one had told us that agents weren't supposed to get any money up front, weren't supposed to be paid until they sold your work. Then they were to take ten percent of whatever the work earned. Ignorance is expensive. That $61.20 was more money back then than my mother paid for a month's rent.

10. I badgered friends and acquaintances into reading my work, and they seemed to like it. Teachers read it and said kindly, unhelpful things. But there were no creative writing classes at my high school, and no useful criticism. At college (in California at that time, junior college was almost free), I took classes taught by an elderly woman who wrote children's stories. She was polite about the science fiction and fantasy that I kept handing in, but she finally asked in exasperation, "Can't you write anything normal?"

A schoolwide contest was held. All submissions had to be made anonymously. My short story won first prize. I was an eighteen-year-old freshman, and I won in spite of competition from older, more experienced people. Beautiful. The $15.00 prize was the first money my writing earned me.

11. After college I did office work for a while, then factory and warehouse work. My size and strength were advantages in factories and warehouses. And no one expected me to smile and pretend I was having a good time.

I got up at two or three in the morning and wrote. Then I went to work. I hated it, and I have no gift for suffering in silence. I muttered and complained and quit jobs and found new ones and collected more rejection slips. One day in disgust I threw them all away. Why keep such useless, painful things?

12. There seems to be an unwritten rule, hurtful and at odds with the realities of American culture. It says you aren't supposed to wonder whether as a Black person, a Black woman, you really might be inferior—not quite bright enough, not quite quick enough, not quite good enough to do the things you want to do. Though, of course, you do wonder. You're supposed to *know* you're as good as anyone. And if you don't know, you aren't supposed to admit it. If anyone near you admits it, you're supposed to reassure them quickly so they'll shut up. That sort of talk is embarrassing. Act tough and confident and don't talk about your doubts. If you never deal with them, you may never get rid of them, but no matter. Fake everyone out. Even yourself.

I couldn't fake myself out. I didn't talk much about my doubts. I wasn't fishing for hasty reassurances. But I did a lot of thinking—the same things over and over.

Who was I anyway? Why should anyone pay attention to what I had to say? Did I have anything to say? I was writing science fiction and fantasy, for God's sake. At that time nearly all professional science-fiction writers were white men. As much as I loved science fiction and fantasy, what was I doing?

Well, whatever it was, I couldn't stop. Positive obsession is about not being able to stop just because you're afraid and full of doubts. Positive obsession is dangerous. It's about not being able to stop at all.

13. I was twenty-three when, finally, I sold my first two short stores. I sold both to writer-editors who were teaching at Clarion, a science-fiction writers' workshop that I was attending. One story was eventually published. The other wasn't. I didn't sell another word for five years. Then, finally, I sold my first novel. Thank God no one told me selling would take so long —not that I would have believed it. I've sold eight novels since then. Last Christmas, I paid off the mortgage on my mother's house.

14. So, then, I write science fiction and fantasy for a living. As far as I know, I'm still the only Black woman who does this. When I began to do a little public speaking, one of the questions I heard most often was, "What good is science fiction to Black people?" I was usually asked this by a Black person. I gave bits and pieces of answers that didn't satisfy me and that probably didn't satisfy my questioners. I resented the question. Why should I have to justify my profession to anyone?

But the answer to that was obvious. There was exactly one other Black science-fiction writer working successfully when I sold my first novel: Samuel R. Delany, Jr. Now there are four of us. Delany, Steven Barnes, Charles R. Saunders, and me. So few. Why? Lack of interest? Lack of confidence? A young Black woman once said to me, "I always wanted to write science fiction, but I didn't think there were any Black women doing it."

Doubts show themselves in all sorts of ways. But still I'm asked, what good is science fiction to Black people?

What good is any form of literature to Black people?

What good is science fiction's thinking about the present, the future, and the past? What good is its tendency to warn or to consider alternative ways of thinking and doing? What good is its examination of the possible effects of science and technology, or social organization and political direction? At its best, science fiction stimulates imagination and creativity. It gets reader and writer off the beaten track, off the narrow, narrow footpath of what "everyone" is saying, doing, thinking—whoever "everyone" happens to be this year.

And what good is all this to Black people?

OCTAVIA E. BUTLER was a renowned writer who received a MacArthur "Genius" Grant and PEN West Lifetime Achievement Award for her body of work. She was the author of several award-winning novels including *Parable of the Sower*, which was a *New York Times* Notable Book of the Year and bestseller. She was acclaimed for her lean prose, strong protagonists, and social observations in stories that range from the distant past to the far future. Sales of her books have increased enormously since her death as the issues she addressed in her Afrofuturistic, feminist novels and short fiction have only become more relevant. She passed away on February 24, 2006.

*Take As Needed

HIROMI GOTO

I cannot offer to you what you have come seeking—because I'm not talking to you in your present. I am talking to a *maybe* you in one of your possible futures. You may never arrive at this imagined place. Godspeed that you don't.

There's nothing I want to share right now about how to write, because after having written and published for over twenty-five years I feel less certain of how I did it than ever before. Many how-to books exist already, in the form of memoirs or creative guidebooks by big-name authors, well-established writer-professors at prestigious writing schools, and radical zinesters. They all have great and not-so-great advice and suggestions, writing exercises, and processes. There are always many, many different ways to achieve a goal or lifelong dream. The only way to "become a writer" is to write. That is all.

But what if you, who once were carried to fantastic worlds, harrowing futures, the depths of hell—to places where yōkai come alive—what if you can no longer find your way there? What if the stories dry up? What then?

What if you not only lose your imagination, but you also *lose faith* in your imagination? What if you turn away from this terrible blankness to seek solace in the stories that other people have written, and discover that you have also lost the desire to read?

I love my mother. She, like many parents everywhere, has offered over the years great and not-so-great advice. Sometimes when I'm feeling vulnerable, I want to hear something comforting from her, but I worry that it may be one of the times when she comes up with less-than-supportive feedback. And so I don't bring all of my troubles to her.

When I finally told her that I can't write like I used to, that my will for it is gone, she said, ohhh, just give it time. You can't draw from the well all the time; you need to replenish it too.

I've stopped reading, I confessed. I can't read novels anymore. (And this felt like a deeper shame, or maybe self-betrayal, than anything else.)

Ohhh, my oka-san said. You're tired of words.

I have returned to the places that nurtured me through childhood—the forests, the wetlands, the seaside, and the rivers. With a camera slung around my neck and a cell phone in my back pocket I wend along paths, observing movements from one season to the next in the cycles of plants from shoot to blossom to seed. The migration of birds. The fruiting of fungi. For these beings are *pre*-word. They are themselves. And I am one self among them. There is no need for a spoken and written human language here. They are their own language. My eyes take in their complex and vibrantly diverse forms. I breathe in deep their perfumes. I listen for the alarm calls of chickadees, squirrels, and thrushes that speak the presence of an owl. I'm nourished by berries both tart and sweet, meaty pine mushrooms, sweet rich chestnuts.

These sites are not free from colonial imperialism. And I'm not an apolitical neutral subject. These are unceded Musqueam, Squamish, and Tseil Waututh Territories. And I am part of a settler population. I carry my own contexts with me when I enter these spaces. How I understand what I observe is filtered through my own cultural frameworks. There is no innocence.

And yet the land holds me, still, as land holds everyone. When I lie back in ocean, she lifts me up. I make sure not to swim too far from shore.

When I'm deep in forest I tip my head back to see the trees standing so tall their tips converge. Bright blue in the spaces between, a promise that rings inside my chest. Raven's sonorous clucks from atop a deadfall. Our eyes meet, then they lift off with a heavy, slow beat of wings.

I find solace in silence. When I say silence, I mean a place that is not intruded upon by human-made sounds. In the city, these sounds, like human language, cannot be escaped.

Solace is necessary when you lose faith. I know better than to seek solace in places that will take more from me than they will give. Alcohol, drugs, gambling, casual sex—it's all fun and games, for a little while. They might distract from the vast emptiness inside of my chest. They might dull the pain or give me a hit of feel-good endorphins. But they won't cure. They will never tell me a good story.

Hayao Miyazaki's 1989 animated film, 魔女の宅急便, or *Kiki's Delivery Service*, as it is known in North America, is based on a novel by Eiko Kadano. Kiki, a young witch, must set off on her own (albeit accompanied by her cat friend, Jiji) at the age of thirteen as a rite of passage. She fulfils her dream of living by the sea and sets up a personal air delivery service—something only she can provide! *Spoiler*: Alas, she loses her powers of flight and falls into a depression. When an older friend comes to visit, Kiki tells her, I used to be able to fly without even thinking about it. Now I'm trying to figure out how I ever did it.

So it is that I find myself, a writer who no longer knows the way back into story.... There is nothing romantic or interesting about a writer who cannot write. It is a cliché, frankly, and writing about not being able to write is a special kind of hell.

Look, you might say, you've written this essay. Yes, yes I have. But I have not written a novel in a very long time. The difference (and I'm not speaking to the skills and challenges of writing a given form, but to my personal process and creative satisfaction) is the difference, for me, between eating at a Japanese restaurant in Canada, and living and eating in Japan. There is an immersiveness to the latter experience that is full-body, full-mind, full-spirit.

And now it is gone.

I cannot tell you how to find your way back because I do not know. I think that it is a very personal crisis that any writer might face, like heroes do when they come to the Great Test. There is a mirror there, and you must see yourself as you are. And then you must find a way through. If you're from a warrior people, maybe you will smash the mirror. Or maybe you will lie down and take a long nap. Maybe you will stare into the mirror for hours, for years, hoping it will disappear .... In whatever form the test takes, you will only find yourself. You will have to find your own way home.

I'm only here to tell you that you are and are not alone. Your struggle is real and terrible, and no one may be able to help you out of this place. And, also, many writers have come to this place before you. And many will arrive long after you are gone.

If you no longer believe in stories, you will not be able to write them. Seek solace in whatever lights up something inside of you. It may be that you will be burdened with this unwanted test for a long time. There are other ways to feel that creative magic you once did. You might find it in different forms. Drawing is a different kind of language—pick up a pencil or ink brush, splash a mark upon paper. Have you fantasized about learning to play a traditional instrument from your culture of origin? You can do it now. Take a long walk beside a salt marsh. Photograph the smallest birds. Plunge a spade into the lawn and dig out all of the sod and start a pollinator's garden.

A small light still burns inside of me. It will not be extinguished; an idea that is hope, an idea that is a need—even if I've lost faith in stories, perhaps stories still have faith in me.

End note: I am beginning to accept that I can't write novels in the ways I did before. There is grief in that. Frustration. Anger. But, also, hope. There are many ways to write a novel … .

HIROMI GOTO is an emigrant from Japan who gratefully lives on the Unceded Musqueam, Skwxwú7mesh, and Tsleil Waututh Territories. Her first novel, *Chorus of Mushrooms*, won the Commonwealth Writers' Prize Best First Book, Canada and Caribbean Region, and was co-winner of the Canada-Japan Book Award. Her second book, *The Kappa Child*, received the James Tiptree Jr. Memorial Award for gender-bending speculative fiction. She's published three novels for children and youth, a book of poetry, and a collection of short stories. Her other honors include the Sunburst Award and the Carl Brandon Parallax Award. *Shadow Life*, her first graphic novel with artist Ann Xu, will be published with First Second Books in early 2021.

Matters of Life and Death

SUSAN PALWICK

There are really only three universal rules of writing:

1. Read.
2. Write.
3. Use what works.

That comes nowhere close to the 1000–1500 words the editors of this volume asked for, though, so I'm going to tell you three stories about my personal rules of writing. Take what you like and leave the rest, as they say in twelve-step groups.

The first story is about motivation. Why do we write? This is a business where it's very easy to lust after the *Big Shinies* ("best of" anthologies! awards! film rights!) and to feel like failures if we don't get them. You may wonder why I'm even in this book; many people have never heard of me.

My first novel, *Flying in Place*, was published in 1992. It's a ghost story about child sexual abuse. It's not autobiographical; I did research and used my imagination. I was afraid someone would tell me I'd gotten everything wrong. Instead, a few months after the book was published, I got a piece of fan mail. It said, "Dear Susan: I was going to kill myself, but then I read your book, and I didn't."

Whenever I feel discouraged about my writing, I remember that letter. If I'd been trying to save someone's life with a story, I never could have done it. I wrote what I had to write, and what I'd written went into the world and did work I never could have planned or expected. I've learned to write, not for the Big Shinies —although they're certainly lovely when they happen—but to allow readers to have relationships with my work. If I'm very lucky, sometimes readers grant me the privilege of telling me about those relationships.

My second story is about process. I've always written slowly, in the sense of having a small output: four novels and two story collections in thirty years. My slow writing used to take the form of writing a story, being paralyzed for two years because I had no ideas, and then writing another story. Wash, rinse, repeat. That was a long time ago, when the field was slightly less dominated by Big Shinies than it is now, but even then, one could attend convention panels on which well-known professionals extolled the necessity of producing a novel a year. I was on one panel where a very pleasant fellow professional recommended writing three or four novels a year.

On that panel, I tried to talk about slow writing as a valid process, but that wasn't what the audience wanted to hear. Since my slowness, at that point, still took the form of frantic bursts of productivity separated by months of anxious despair (will I ever write again? will I ever have another idea? will anyone ever buy more of my work?), I could hardly blame them.

Then I found a much better way to be a slow writer.

I started weaving and spinning. (I strongly recommend having some tactile, hands-on creative pursuit to balance out the interior work of writing, but that's another essay.) Spinning involves taking a bunch of raw fluffy wool, lengthening the fluff by stretching it—a process called *drafting*—and twisting the wool to strengthen it, creating a thread.

When I first started spinning, I used a drop spindle, because spinning wheels seemed insanely expensive. (I now have two. Don't even ask how many looms I have.) The women at my weaving guild told me, "They're called drop spindles because people drop them so often." The spindle drops when the thread breaks, and the thread breaks when the spinner hasn't yet mastered the proper ratio of draft to twist.

I was struggling to master this arcane skill when a more experienced spinner, watching me, said kindly, "You're drafting too fast." She meant that I'd stretched out the wool too much without twisting to lock it into place, resulting in my thread breaking and my drop spindle landing on the floor yet again.

But writers talk about drafting too, and a light bulb went off. I'd been struggling to write stories more quickly. Trying to recreate a few glorious experiences where I'd written a story in one or two sittings, I'd write several thousand words in a burst, only to find myself with no idea what to say next. The story would languish for months or years while I fretted. Would I ever write again? Would I ever have another idea?

What if I'd been drafting too fast? What if, instead of pushing myself to write more quickly, I deliberately wrote more slowly?

I decided to write 500 words a day. I'd stop after 500 words even if I knew what came next, instead of writing to the end of what I knew in one sitting.

The first story I wrote this way flowed more easily than any story had in years. It sold almost immediately to *Asimov's* and was selected for the inaugural volume of *The Best American Science Fiction and Fantasy* from Houghton Mifflin. Shiny!

I'm still not an overflowing fountain of publications (much less Big Shinies), but it turns out that around 500 words a day is a very comfortable pace for me, especially when I have a project already underway. I can usually write that much in half an hour or so. I can sustain this small daily discipline even when I'm working, even when I'm traveling or have house guests, even when I'm so exhausted that I'm literally nodding off over the keyboard. Sometimes the words aren't very good, but they're there, waiting to be edited, and 500 words a day allows my thinking process to keep up with my writing. Plot ideas and epiphanies seem to emerge organically as I write, rather than having to be mined with pickaxes.

This practice turns writing into an everyday activity, both as ordinary and as essential as feeding my cats or brushing my teeth. Keeping the work low pressure has made writing more fun, and actually increased my output.

Now for the third story. Back when I was still an English professor, I taught a fiction workshop where students kept killing off their characters. Some of them did this because they were stumped about how to end their stories, and "suddenly the sun went nova and they all died" solved the problem. Some did it to make the story seem more serious. Some did it to make the story seem more shocking. What troubled me most was that too many of these dead characters went unmourned even within their own fictional universes. Most of the corpses were plot devices or window dressing.

I talked to my students about this problem. I urged them to keep their characters alive, but the body count inexorably mounted. After several more weeks of this, I announced in frustration that I was giving a final exam. Any student who'd killed off a character had to write a eulogy for that character and read it aloud at our last class meeting.

Because of the structure of my course contract, I really had no way to enforce this, and my students knew it. Nonetheless, my announcement had a remarkable effect. A record number of resurrections occurred in revision. In workshop stories, characters seemingly marked for certain doom enjoyed miraculous near misses. The number of gory mass murders plummeted, and for the rest of the semester, the story endings were more thoughtful and nuanced.

Some characters stayed dead, though. To my pleasure, the students honored our agreement and showed up at our final-exam session with eulogies in hand. Some were funny. Some were deeply moving. All revealed much more about those characters than we'd learned in the stories where they originally appeared.

I don't know if this exercise made my students, from then on, think twice when they considered killing a character. I hope so. What I wanted them to learn is that everyone has a life, even if you'll never know it. Everyone has a story, and even if you don't care about telling that story in your story, someone else in the story should know it. Even if you don't grieve your dead characters, someone in your story should.

Remember Tolkien's Samwise Gamgee, in Ithilien, coming across the dead Southron slain by Faramir's men, and wondering who he was and what had brought him there? That scene is a perfect example.

So, here are my three personal rules for writing:

1. Remember that writing can save lives.
2. Make your writing an everyday part of your life.
3. Honor the lives in your writing.

But if this doesn't make sense to you? If I'm not important enough to listen to, because I haven't collected enough Big Shinies? Then, at least: Read. Write. And use what works.

SUSAN PALWICK was a student at Clarion West in 1985 and filled in as a last-minute instructor in 2015, after Connie Willis was bitten by a bat and couldn't teach. Everyone involved survived. Susan has published four novels with Tor and two story collections, one with Tachyon and one with Fairwood. She was a founding editor of NYRSF and taught literature and writing for twenty years at the University of Nevada, Reno, retiring in 2017 to get a Masters in Social Work. Despite having been scolded by many editors and fellow writers for not being more prolific, Susan has won the Rhysling, Alex, and Crawford Awards, and has been shortlisted for the World Fantasy, Mythopoeic, and Philip K. Dick. She lives with her husband and three cats in Reno, where she now works as a hospital chaplain and continues to write very slowly.

Proverbs of Hell for Writers

IAN MCDONALD

> "... which the world shall have whether they will or no."
>
> —WILLIAM BLAKE.

1. Look it up.

2. If you're not reading, you're not writing.

3. Whose story is this?

4. Your reading time is as sacrosanct as your writing time.

5. Read plays. Dialogue is much more about how people talk than what people say.

6. Read your dialogue aloud. Remember where you tried to breathe.

7. No one wants to read your Dungeons and Dragons campaign. Really.

8. If not for these characters, at this place and time, this story would never have happened.

9. In conversation, no one ever listens to anyone else. We're all waiting for a gap in the voices to speak our own minds. Conversations are broken, partial. They veer off at strange tangents.

10. Fold your arms. Which arm is uppermost? Now fold them the other way. Interesting and uncomfortable, isn't it? When we write we tend to have a dominant sense. It's good to shift to another sense for that exquisite feeling of fresh discomfort.

11. Read outside your comfort zone. Read widely, read expecting to be surprised. Read with an open mind and heart.

12. Kill snappy dialogue. You're not in a sitcom. Imagine how hellish life would be if you were.

13. No one likes a wisecracker.

14. Try and get some exercise. If only because it's the kind of welcome distraction that frees up real thinking.

15. You need to surprise yourself. You need that shock of "where did *that* come from?"

16. The drudgery of the pen is still drudgery.

17. What's meant is never said. What's said is never meant.

18. Creativity is not soul-force and cannot be summoned by willpower.

19. What if humans do not have hidden depths? What if we are wide, connected shallow lagoons?

20. If you ask, what do my characters want from this situation, you must do the same for your relationship with social media.

21. Avoid Freud.

22. On that, recognize nineteenth-century ideas on psychology, economics, creativity, art for what they are: from three centuries ago.

23. Imagine being marooned with your protagonist for eleven hours in a crowded airport.

24. There is a sweet spot, that when you hit it, is the finest thing. That spot is so hard to find, but it's strong drugs.

25. The triumph and tragedy of novels are that they speak strongest about individuals, to individuals.

26. There is no such thing as a bad idea. There are, however, badly worked ideas.

27. Who's hurting here?

28. We read fiction because it's better than the real thing.

29. You use 20 percent of your research, but unless you do it all, you won't know which 20 percent.

30. What do you take for granted in your world? So will your characters in their world.

31. There is no such thing as inspiration.

32. Creativity is putting things together. Sometimes those things have never been together before.

33. There are other ways of telling stories than the western three-act paradigm. Discover them. They all have strength, value, and virtue. All are very much worth learning.

34. You can't edit a blank page.

35. All we can write about is people, not groups.

36. Creativity is play.

37. There is no success without luck. But you can work your luck.

38. It's never about the ideas. The universe is full of ideas. They fall like raindrops.

39. You don't need anyone else's ideas. You'll never use all the ones you have.

40. It's all about the execution.

41. Only the smallest of souls gets hung up on POV.

42. Everything that rough guides say is creativity is not. This included.

43. Find your time, however long or short. Defend it like a hilltop.

44. Answers come when you look away from the questions.

45. No villain believes they're a villain.

46. If in doubt, cut it out.

47. That bit you notice that makes your frontal lobes bleed every time you read it: you think no one else will notice it. They will. If you can see it, everyone can see it.

48. You can be smart, but never be clever. No one likes clever.

49. If you worry about likable characters, how likable is your best friend? Your mother? Your life partner? Your child?

50. Don't make yourself hate it. It's all too easy to hate it.

51. No one's impressed by your word count.

52. Whoever came up with "pantser vs. plotter" needs the harshest of punishments. Primarily for being someone involved in writing who came up with as ugly a word as *pantser*.

53. In general, avoid apostrophes in alien names. Very few westerners know how to pronounce them.

54. Turn up for work. By that I mean, even on the worst, sickest, most hungover, darkest, dreariest days when you can't spit out a syllable, just open up whatever you write in/on/with and look at your work. That counts.

55. Check other cultures' naming conventions.

56. Care about the words. Care about their weight, feel, rhythm, sound, what other words they sit with.

57. Plot versus language is a false dichotomy.

58. Titles either come at once or not at all.

59. Skunk cabbage is not native to Britain.

60. The brilliance of ideas colliding outshines a million suns.

61. A character doesn't have to be likable. They do have to be compelling.

62. It's not about you.

63. It's certainly not about me.

64. Start each day reading what you wrote the previous day. After a few lines you'll go hmmn, then change a word here, a clause there. Then whole sentences, deleted, changed, moved. By the time you get to the end, you're ready to glide into today's work.

65. Listen more than you speak.

66. Care about language. An architect cares about the materials that go into a building. Each has its quality and virtue.

67. Latinisms kill.

68. E-Prime is a version of English without the verb *to be*, in any of its forms. It's a refreshing way to look at your writing. It sits down hard on passives like "is sitting," "is writing," as opposed to "sits," "writes." It liquidates certainties of making one thing equal to another: "the writer is Irish" vs. "the Irish writer."

69. "Write what you know" is that most damnable of lies because there is a vein of truth through it. The best writing transcends the constraints put around it. All great books break at least one law.

70. All that needs to be said about "said" has been said.

71. Think about voice. Before anything.

72. Do you laugh? Do you cry? Do you feel horny, shaky, disturbed?

73. The wonder of it is: these words came at this time, in this place and are frozen into a document. At another time and place, they would have been other words.

74. I come with terrible news: the universe is purposeless and hostile. It has no meaning, it has no narrative. Humans crave narrative. Narrative is a purely human creation. Where we see a narrative, a story: someone made that. That is why the only useful skill writers have is the ability to spot someone making up a story.

75. I like actors. Really. I like theater. To me, acting and writing are sides of a coin. One takes the physical, emotional world and puts it onto paper as words. The other takes the words from the paper and puts them into the world.

76. You're writing characters, not advocates.

77. Irony is pareidolia. It's Jesus in the tortilla.

78. Writing a scene is like a bad party. Arrive as late as is polite and leave as early as possible.

79. Take delight in things. Especially small things.

80. Never be afraid. Fear kills writing with one blow.

81. Ask questions. Listen to the answers.

82. Ask questions of yourself first. Listen to the answers.

83. We all have biases that shape our writing. The political ones are the easiest. The personal, historical, emotional ones are subtler. My characters never dance.

84. I know a dozen authentic recipes for ragù Bolognese.

85. You owe respect to your sources, your guides: whatever, whoever, wherever, whenever they are. Remember it every time you crank up the words.

86. You may very well not be a moral person. If you disagree, tell me what it is you do when you write?

87. Combat veterans are treating PTSD with psilocybin. Shrooms. Are they right? Is it moral? If not, why not?

88. Martin Amis writes of the "War Against Cliché."

89. Everything is a small world, everywhere is a walled city.

90. Never let anyone who isn't a writer tell you about writing.

91. Talent borrows, genius steals. I stole this.

92. The popular view of writing — of many arts — is still Victorian, mired in Romanticism. That needs to die, starving, consumptive, alone in a freezing garret. As language is the thing that connects us, writing must be social, connected, powered by dozens — hundreds — of lives and stories and ways of being human.

93. Every novel, every story is a map of the human heart.

94. Only connect.

IAN MCDONALD is a (mostly) SF writer living in Northern Ireland, just outside Belfast. A Hugo winner, he's been nominated for almost all major SFF Awards. He's been published in fifteen languages. His first novel, *Desolation Road*, was published to acclaim in 1988 and has recently been reprinted as a Gollancz Masterwork. His most recent books are *Luna: Moon Rising*, the conclusion to the Luna Trilogy, and *The Menace from Farside*, a Tor.com novella. He's taught Clarion West twice, in 2010 and 2014.

A note about the Clarion West Writers Workshop

The mission of Clarion West is to support emerging and under-represented voices by providing writers with world-class instruction to empower their creation of wild and amazing worlds and, through conversation and public engagement, to bring those voices to an ever-expanding community.

Clarion West began as a six-week residential workshop, and that continues to be the organization's flagship event; however, one-day in-person workshops and a variety of online classes, workshops, panels, and community-building opportunities are now also offered throughout the year.

Regarding the big six-week workshop — the first thing you should know is that you don't need to attend any workshop to "make it" as a writer. There is no guarantee that anyone will succeed — by whatever definition of success they choose — and for those who do, the only essential experience contributing to their success is that they write, write, write.

The workshop is held annually in Seattle, generally from mid-June to the end of July, in a secret location near the University of Washington. For six weeks, eighteen students occupy a single house or dormitory wing, where they read, write, eat, sleep, sweat, suffer, and bond. Every week, each student writes a story, so every week, each student also reads and critiques their seventeen classmates' stories. And each week, a different instructor — a science fiction, fantasy, or horror author or editor — joins the students to guide critique sessions (traditionally using the Milford system, although the workshop is exploring alternate models), teach elements of story writing, and impart writerly wisdom.

The workshop, like this book, is not for beginning writers. Neither is it for advanced writers (although a few professionals have attended). The writers most suited for this workshop are in the liminal space of having worked long and hard to prove — to themselves, first and foremost — that they are devoted to writing, but who are still discovering how to break into professional spaces: writers who are ready for a giant leap forward and a commitment to their writing career.

The workshop is an opportunity to learn. You will learn about writing, about stories, about the greater speculative fiction community, and about yourself. You will most likely become a better writer. (You may also decide that writing is not the career for you.) But the workshop cannot *make* you a writer; it can only help you shape and develop the writer that you already are.

The workshop is also an opportunity to develop lasting relationships with a group of your peers and industry professionals. With six weeks to get to know your classmates —and their writing styles, particular strengths, and areas of insight—we hope you'll build lifelong friendships and leave with dedicated critique partners. Someone in the workshop will love everything you write and be your hype person; someone will have a critical eye for your weak points and be your best editor. We may write alone, but we flourish in community.

Full details of the application process are available at clarionwest.org, but in brief, the application consists of a short personal statement, up to thirty pages of your best fiction prose (one story, multiple shorter stories, or an excerpt of a longer work), and an application fee. Substantial scholarships are available, so while there are many valid reasons *not* to attend the workshop, tuition generally need not be one of them. Writers identifying as BIPOC, LGBTQIA+, or disabled, or who are otherwise marginalized, are particularly encouraged to apply.

Good luck!

Acknowledgements

We are ever grateful to the many people who have helped ensure the success of this book. In particular, thanks to Nancy Kress for pointers and advice during early plotting and planning stages; Eileen Gunn for marketing advice as well as keen titling and design insights; John D. Berry for the flawless interior and cover designs; Cory Skerry for the lovely and whimsical cover art; Kate Dieda for proofreading assistance; Mary and Fred Gentry for contract advice; Workshop Administrator Jae Steinbacher for helping us write the closing note about Clarion West; Development and Outreach Coordinator Evan J. Peterson and Executive Director Marnee Chua for their brilliant work publicizing the book; the estates of Octavia E. Butler, Ursula K. Le Guin, and Vonda N. McIntyre for allowing their words to live on in this volume; all of the instructors who so graciously entrusted us to share their wisdom with the world; to the generations of Clarion West instructors and students who've shaped the program and made the organization what it is today; and especially to Vonda, without whom none of this would have happened.

About the Editors

TOD MCCOY is a writer and editor whose work has appeared in *Asimov's*, *Starward Tales II*, *The People's Apocalypse*, *Bronies: For the Love of Ponies*, and other publications. He graduated from the Clarion West Writers Workshop in 2010 and is currently the chair of the Clarion West board, as well as the publisher of Hydra House Books. He lives outside Missoula where he accidentally snubbed James Lee Burke at the post office.

M. "HUW" EVANS is a sometime writer, an increasingly frequent editor, an ex-physician pathologist, an always dad, a dog's reluctant person, a reliable-if-uninspiring cook, and, most recently, a creator of magic wands. He's published one story, *Nine Instances of Rain* (workshopped with Connie Willis and titled by Neile Graham), in *Giganotosaurus*. Huw has resided for at least three months straight in each of the following: Louisiana, New Mexico, Nicaragua, Oregon, the Philippines, Switzerland, and Iain M. Banks's Culture universe. One of those strikes Huw as the ideal place for his daughters to grow up—but Seattle, his home, is a close second.

BOOK DESIGN BY JOHN D. BERRY. The text typefaces used are Quadraat and Quadraat Sans, designed by Fred Smeijers. Quadraat is a thoroughly digital typeface, with qualities that are rooted in sixteenth-century type. Its narrow, slightly slanted italic comes from the writing traditions of Renaissance Italy and serves as a clear contrast to the roman type. Quadraat Sans is a humanist sans serif with its own distinct character, as well as a natural affinity for its serif sibling. Display typefaces used on the cover are variations of Roslindale, designed by David Jonathan Ross and inspired by the nineteenth-century DeVinne types, named after the famed American printer.

CPSIA information can be obtained
at www.ICGtesting.com
Printed in the USA
LVHW030813010221
677983LV00006B/278